PROCESS

PROCESS
TO PROFIT

SYSTEMISE YOUR BUSINESS TO BUILD
A HIGH PERFORMING TEAM AND GAIN
MORE TIME, MORE CONTROL AND MORE PROFIT

MARIANNE PAGE

RƎTHINK PRESS

First published in 2013 by Rethink Press
(www.rethinkpress.com)

To Mum and Dad
Wish you were here to see this

To Sas, bright, crazy and always honest
Thanks for putting up with me

To those who've helped me become who I am
You know who you are

xxxx

Praise for
Process to Profit

My first job was at McDonald's. From age 15 to 17, I worked the same systems that were being used world-wide by the most famously successful franchise on Earth. This experience set me up for a successful career in business because I saw first hand the power of passionate people working a proven process.

When I read Marianne's book I was delighted that someone had translated the essence of McDonald's success for other businesses. No matter what you think of the burgers and fries, the business is remarkable and you can learn a lot from them. Read this book if you dream of having a business that runs like clockwork and keeps people engaged and passionate for decades.

Daniel Priestley, Entrepreneur, international speaker and best-selling author of 'Entrepreneur Revolution'

Marianne gives you the formula for working smarter not harder! Without doubt a must read for anyone looking to grow a successful business.

Patrick Milenuszkin, Founder of Brand New Vision

If this book doesn't convince you of the importance of systems and processes in growing a profitable business then I'm not sure what will. Marianne clearly knows this territory inside out and has loaded the book with actionable tips and strategies that you can implement to start reaping the rewards in your business today.

Kelly Clifford, Founder of Profit in Focus and best-selling author of 'Profit Rocket'

'Process to Profit' is THE essential handbook for everyone from the entrepreneur to the medium-sized business.

Marianne deftly walks you through the steps needed to perfect your processes, engage your people for success and platform your business for effortless expansion.

If you want to increase the value you deliver to your customers while slashing expenditure and boosting your profits, this is the book for you.

Liz Hopkin, Black Belt Six Sigma

'Process to Profit' is a comprehensive piece on building a solid business. It approaches the topic in a holistic manner, dealing with the many facets of business that each one of us must master to succeed. Both seasoned and budding entrepreneurs alike will draw gems from this book, I certainly did. Read it … and read it again.

Marcus Ubl, Co-Founder Entrevo Global

A little gem of well-structured advice to take new and experienced business owners through a journey that will improve their understanding of business and ultimately increase profits. This book encourages the reader to think about their own business as they work through the tips, guidance and anecdotes and there are plenty of pauses for reflection. I gained a lot of insight about the way I work now and used the exercises to help me to discover ways of treating my customers so well that they will never want to leave me.

Janette Eustace, CEO, Business Perspective

Contents

Introduction

A BRIGHT FUTURE

was taught the importance of the customer from a very early age. Not quite as early as my dad, his first job was selling sticks off the back of his horse-drawn cart at the age of seven, but early enough. As young assistants' for his coal merchant business, my sisters and I would take customer orders over the telephone: 'Is that "best coal", madam?' and collect money from customers who came to the front door.

During these early years, I was taught the importance of building good relationships with your customers; of giving a little for free when customers were wavering, or maybe times were hard; of giving them a quality product and up-selling when times were good; of giving them a fair price, and friendly, reliable service. In a nutshell, I was taught that if your customers *know*, *like*, and *trust* you, they will stay with you for life.

was taught to have a passion for my customers and a determination to look after and develop those who worked for me, without ever forgetting that the underlying purpose of any business is to make a profit.

Passion + People = Profit

I learned the power of process and systems a little later in life, as a graduate trainee with 'The most successful small business in the world'.

McDonald's, like many other large corporations, may polarise views, but it's easy to forget that they are a corporation made up of thousands of small businesses, and their undeniable success as a brand and a business has been built on the foundations of strong leadership, committed relationships, investment in the development of every individual, and systems. Quite simply, McDonald's have a system and a process for everything.

Systems run the business; People run the systems.

It was during my years with McDonald's that I learned how to develop logical, repeatable systems, how to root out inefficiency and duplication, and keep my bit of the business running like a well-oiled machine. I learned the importance of engaging and developing your team to work the systems effectively, while keeping everyone focused on the customer and the need for continuous improvement.

In short, I learned that Systems run the business; People run the systems. It's the foundation for business growth and it's the reason I started my own usiness, Bright. I knew that I could add value by elping business owners not only to understand this, ut to build the processes and systems that would be he springboard for their future growth and success.

ystems matter. Systems to help you hire, develop nd keep the right people. Systems to help you find, ook after and keep the right customers. The most uccessful companies, big and still growing, recognise this, and have process and systems in every rea of their business.

Passion + People + Process = Profit

'm sure that you are passionate about what you do. And that if you could, you would probably do everything yourself to make sure that it was done right. But you can't; there are only 24 hours in a day, and ven the most driven individuals need to sleep.

he trouble is that sometimes we have great people, but they just aren't clear about their role or what hey are expected to do, so we end up running a usiness that is more like Wacky Races – everyone oing in roughly the same direction, but in their wn way and at their own speed – than Formula One – a well drilled, high performing team in which very member knows their role and how it fits into he bigger picture.

To build your revenue you have to give your customers a great experience that brings together three key elements within your business:

1. Your **Passion** and your belief in a customer first culture
2. Great **People** who love giving their customers a great experience… and
3. **Process** and systems that make it easy for your people to give your customer the consistency they're looking for.

Revenue won't build if costs aren't controlled effectively.

Service excellence can't be achieved without efficient systems to support it and great people to work the systems.

Bring these elements together and you'll find that not only do you have more time and more control of your business, but that you also have more profit and better cash flow to fund your growth.

MORE TIME, MORE CONTROL, MORE PROFIT

You may be reading this book because you are already a successful business owner. Maybe you've grown from the one-man band you started with and now find yourself with a team, a group of loyal customers and a pretty ok turnover. So, life is good, right?

Or it would be, if only you had half-decent cash-flow, more profit, and time to enjoy and build on your initial success.

Instead...

As the team has grown, so has your workload.

You feel that you have to check up all the time.

You've become less efficient.

Your costs have gone up.

Your profits have tumbled.

You think customers might be leaving you, but you're not sure if, or why.

You have good people but you just don't trust them to do the job as you would.

You have less and less time to spend with your family and friends.

You're working harder and harder, but you're just not seeing the results.

You have big plans for the business, but if it means even more work for you, you know you'll either crack up, or damage your closest relationships. Maybe both.

You're not leaping out of bed every morning, full of enthusiasm for the day ahead like you used to.

Great news:

You've just reached the Great Awakening. That time in every small business owner's life when they realise that hard work alone does not lead to business success; that if they want things to be different, they're going to have to do things differently; if they want to grow their business, they're going to have improve their cashflow and improve their profit; that things need to change.

Welcome to a bright new world!

In just picking up this book you've shown your willingness to invest your very precious time, and taken that all-important first step towards growing your business. Trust me, it's going to be worth the effort.

Hard work alone does not lead to business success.

I'm going to show you how process and systems can dramatically improve your revenue and reduce your costs, and then I'm going to help you to develop the process and systems that are right for your business right now.

In return, I need you to be honest with yourself; I need you to be willing to change what needs to be changed, however well it served you in the past; and I need you to be willing to invest the time and effort that will be required to make the changes, and reap the rewards.

In Part 1, we'll look at your current situation, and our passion for your business

In Part 2, we'll cover the process and systems that will help you to make more money

In Part 3, we'll look at the process and systems that will save you money

In Part 4, we'll talk about your key business numbers and the process for staying on top of them

In Part 5, we'll discover the importance of culture and leadership in growing a successful business

So, what are we waiting for?

Go get your drink of choice and a comfy chair, grab our notepad, iPad or laptop ready to make yourself ome notes, and let's take a 'no holds barred' ride through your business.

"The measure of intelligence is the ability to change."
ALBERT EINSTEIN

5 KEY POINTS TO REMEMBER

1. Systems run the business; People run the Systems.

2. Successful companies have process and systems in every area of their business.

3. To build your revenue you must give your customer a great experience.

4. Process and systems will dramatically improve your revenue and reduce your costs.

5. You need to be willing to invest time and effort to make changes.

PART ONE

Grow Your Business – It Starts With You

"Your future is only as bright
as your mind is open."

RICH WILKINS

WHERE ARE YOU NOW?

f you want to lose weight, you start by getting on he scales.

efore you can decide where you want to be and ow we're going to get you there, I really need you o think about where you are now: a starting point o measure success against later. What state is your usiness in: where are you at with cashflow, profit-bility, your customer experience? What are the sues? What's working, and what's not?

need you to spend a little time working out how ou really feel about your business right now. low's your passion and desire? How much do you eally want this?

What's your 'why?'

What gets you out of bed in the morning and keeps ou going until late in the evening?

it money? No shame in that if it is. We all need noney to survive, to keep our family safe, to enjoy he good things in life. We need profit to keep our usiness moving, to keep it growing, to keep our mployees in jobs. We need cashflow to fund our rowth. So, it's ok to want to make money; it loesn't make you a bad person!

Is it the challenge? Challenging yourself to do more than you thought possible; to prove others wrong; to make your parents or your family proud?

Is it to help others?

To build relationships?

Or because you just *love* helping people and making their lives a little bit easier?

'Loving to help people' sounds a bit cheesy, doesn't it? And yet it may be the one reason for being in business that makes the difference between being average and a huge success.

> **Big businesses have been built by people who had a greater passion for what they were giving their customers than what they were getting from them in return.**

If you look around at some of the big businesses today, and research into the motives of those who built them, you might be surprised to find that they have been built by people who had a greater passion for what they were giving their customers -their product, their service, their idea – than what they were getting from them in return. Richard Branson (Virgin), Steve Jobs (Apple), Mike Harris (First Diect, Egg), Anita Roddick (Bodyshop) are some of the most high profile examples of this, but there will be others, some of whom you may know personally.

These are people who are naturally tuned into the message first brought to us by Napoleon Hill (author of *Think And Grow Rich*) and summed up so well in that lovely little parable, *The Go Giver* (Burg and Mann), which builds on Hill's belief that people do business with, and refer business to, those who they know, like and trust.

Written as a parable about Joe, the ambitious young go-getter, *The Go Giver* can at times get a little mushy, as parables often do. But the messages are simple yet powerful, and certainly made me think about the way I want to do business.

The Go Giver has at its heart, four key principles, or 'Laws':

The Law of Value: Your true worth is determined by how much more you give in value than take in payment. Ask yourself these questions about your business: does it serve; does it add value to others; and only then, does it make money?

The Law of Compensation: Your income is determined by how many people you serve and how well you serve them. As you can always find more people to serve, there is no limitation on what you can earn.

The Law of Influence: Your influence is determined by how abundantly you place other people's interests first. This law tells you to forget about 50:50, forget about win-win, and focus fully on the other person's win. It points out that what makes people attractive, magnetic even, is that they love to give. Givers attract, and have an army of personal ambassadors, who then want to see them succeed. It's a powerful concept.

The Law of Receptivity: The key to effective giving is to stay open to receiving. Continuously learning, having big dreams, being curious and having self-belief, are all ways that we can be receptive. And finally...

The Law of Authenticity: The most valuable gift you have to offer is yourself. As Burg and Mann say, 'No matter what your training, no matter what your skills, no matter what area you're in, *you* are your most important commodity. The most valuable gift you have to offer is you.' A great message for us and for everyone in our team, and a direct contradiction of the message from the carpetbaggers of get rich quick schemes.

> When someone's motivation is to make things better for people and solve their problem, their business is going to be successful.

When someone's motivation is to help, serve, make things better for people and solve their problem, their business is going to be successful.

So, what's *your* motivation for being in business?

And while we're at it, here's another deep and meaningful question, which I make no excuses for, since it should be something we are able to answer in life and in business:

What do you want to be known for?

When people are standing by your graveside, or holding your little urn in their hands, what do you want them to be saying about you?

Is it that you had heaps of integrity, that you always kept your promises big and small, and never let anybody down?

Is it that you went out of your way to find solutions for customers, enjoying the challenge to you and your team, and always, Hannibal-like, either found a way, or built one?

Maybe you were great at adding value, surprising your customers with added touches, unexpected discounts and freebies, thinking about what was important to them, what they needed at any given point.

Or could it be that your people always believed that you wanted them to be the best they could be. That you had fun with them, invested in their development, in their dreams and ambitions, giving them work and life skills that kept them loyal to you and your business, but also set them up to have fulfilling lives?

> **To grow your business successfully, you need to have a very clear picture of why you're in business.**

In order to grow your business successfully, you need to have a very clear picture of why you're in business and what you want to be known for, and people need to be at the centre of both answers. Because business is pretty much all about people and relationships.

HOW'S YOUR BUSINESS DOING?

"In order to move forward into the future, you need to know where you've been."

CHARLES WILLIAMS

Every business has the same foundations for success – growth, profitability and cashflow. It's possible to have one without the others, but to be successful these three foundations of your business must be robust and healthy.

It's how an accountant would look at your business, with their main focus being:

Is your business going to grow?
Is it going to make a profit?
Does it have good cashflow?

o answer those questions they will look at your
evenue drivers, and your costs – what's making
ou money, and what's costing you money – in the
our key areas that impact your growth, profitability
nd cashflow:

Your Service and Branded Customer Experience
Your People – administration and management
Your Operations
Your Financial Controls

or many businesses, it's largely luck if they're prof-
able or have good growth, as they haven't mapped
ut their customer experience, so they don't know
vhere the gaps are; they haven't trained their staff or
iven them great systems to work with; they haven't
dentified inefficiencies in their operation and de-
ised solutions for them; and they don't know their
umbers, so their financial controls are poor.

s luck will only take you so far, let's take a bit of
ime to think about *your* business.

Ve'll go through these areas in much more detail
ater, but for now, I just want you to have a feel for
he type of experience you're currently giving your
ustomers and how your operation is running.

Your Customer Experience

How would you rate it on a scale of 1-10? How would your customers rate it? If you don't know, then there's your first gap. Do you have a good service system for your team to follow? Do you think that you might be missing out on sales due to gaps in your systems? Do you have the right people serving your customers – people who enjoy serving?

Your People

And what about your people? Do you know if you have the right number with the right skills in your business? Do you have a training programme that they all go through? Do they get regular coaching and feedback so that they know how they're doing and what standards you expect? Do they have simple and effective systems to follow in order to do the job right first time?

How would your customers rate your business?

Your Operation

Is your operation efficient? If you had to rate it on a scale from Wacky Races through to Formula One, where would it sit? Are you organised and well-drilled? Does everyone know their role and how it fits into the bigger picture? Are you using technology and equipment that is up to date, fit for purpose and which works well together?

Your Financial Controls

How well do you know your business numbers beyond revenue, cashflow and profitability? Could you answer questions about the sales of different products, how many customers you've gained in the last twelve months, how many you've lost in the last three? Do you know what brings in the main 80% of your income? And what's costing you more to produce or stock than it makes you in sales?

It's important at this point to be honest with yourself about where you are now, and to begin to see that there may be inefficiencies or opportunities that we can exploit to make your business stronger and help it to grow.

Based on this snapshot of where you are now, what are the top three problems that you want to address?

.

.

.

WHERE DO YOU WANT TO BE?

Great stuff. You now have a good, up to date feel for where your business is at, what's working for you and what's not. It's not a detailed review, but at this point all we're after is a gut feel for where the opportunities and inefficiencies sit, so that you can focus on those particular areas as you go through

the book. And we know what your top three problems are. Perfect. We'll review how you feel about
those when we get to the end of the book.

What we need to get you to think about now is
where you want to be.

How do you want to feel about your business?

What are you looking for in terms of cashflow and
profitability?

Do you want more time, more control?

Stop reading and take some time to think about this.

Think about what that ideal future looks like for
you. What does it sound like? What does it feel like?

Don't pick up the book again until you're happy
that you can answer these questions, because you
know what they say:

"If you don't know where you're going you might end up some place else."
YOGI BERRA

So now you know where you are, and you know
where you want to be, the big question to answer is
what's stopping you?

eally? What is stopping you from getting to your
deal?

s it something real, like a lack of skill or knowledge?

Or something self-imposed like a fear of failure?

Are you telling yourself you don't have time to do
what needs to be done, or is it that you can't figure
out what needs to be done?

Again, take a bit of time to get some clarity around
his and write your thoughts down. At the end of
he book we'll come back to see if what you have
written down still exists as a block for you.

UNBLOCKING YOUR PATH

The Simple Power of Systems and Process

I've talked to a lot of entrepreneurs over the years
and for every one of them the growth and scalability
of their business is pretty close to the top of their
minds. Their thoughts turn to funding, to adding
staff and improving leadership skills, maybe to
product creation, but while these are all important
considerations for any successful business, what is
often missed is the need to create the systems which
will form the platform for growth.

While it is true that many small businesses are run
instinctively, with a small team who simply 'make

things happen' – maybe because they have been there from the start, this modus operandi will ultimately fall short as new employees are brought in to deal with new business.

So it makes sense to start thinking along the lines of how you might set up your business as a franchise, even if you have no desire to scale your business in this way. Thinking about what you would need to have in place to make sure everything was consistent, no matter where that second or third franchise was, is a great starting point for thinking about systems and process.

Give yourself the chance to take full advantage of the opportunities that come your way.

The first few years of a business are exciting and filled with opportunity, but they can also be stressful and at times a little chaotic, with many a business owner feeling like they have no time and even less control. By investing time early in building a solid foundation of systems and procedures, you give yourself the chance to take full advantage of the opportunities that come your way, and you may be able to sleep just that little bit better at night, knowing that you are prepared for whatever comes.

THE POWER OF PROCESS AND GOOD SYSTEMS

Iffective process and systems can have a hugely ositive effect on you and your business, and form a trong foundation for sustainable growth. Here are ist some of the benefits.

Iaking your life easier

OOD SYSTEMS FREE UP YOUR TIME

Your hiring system will help you to hire the right people first time. A robust and simple system in which you are fully involved will deliver great results and mean less time and money wasted in removing poor choices, and having to re-hire.

Your people development system will ensure that everyone knows their job, which means that you don't have to watch over them. Your team and your managers are empowered to make decisions, which means fewer decisions for you, and those you do have to make are quicker and easier.

OOD SYSTEMS GIVE YOU CONFIDENCE IN YOUR TEAM

Think about your team right now: is it Wacky Races, or Formula One? Good systems lead to a well-drilled team who know what they are doing and deliver both quality and speed.

When you've trained your people well, and given them great process and systems, you don't need to be there for your business to run smoothly.

Your team are fully engaged and your performance management system keeps them focused.

- Individuals take responsibility for their own job
  and understand they are accountable if they don't
  follow the system. They feel empowered, and that
  applies self-imposed pressure to deliver.

- New employees learn much more easily, and can
  be trusted on their own much sooner.

GOOD SYSTEMS OPEN UP THE OPPORTUNITY TO FRANCHISE YOUR BUSINESS

- A system for every area of your business is a
  franchising model.

- Systems can easily be replicated, just as they are
  easily learned by your team.

- Most systems can also be translated, so it's possible to think on a global scale if that's your goal.

GOOD SYSTEMS HELP YOU TO DEVELOP YOUR PEOPLE AS PEOPLE

- The empowerment that comes from your systems allows your team to grow and develop as
  people as well as employees.

- They know that you will support risk-taking and
  that they will make the right decisions if they
  think Customer and System first.

- You are not looking over their shoulder because
  you have confidence that they know their role, and
  that in turn builds their confidence and self-belief.

- Once your team are fully-trained you will delegate responsibilities to them and, while you will

always follow-up, you will no longer need to check-up on them.

Every system and every procedure is documented and can be picked up more easily as a result, so every member of your team has the opportunity to learn every system and rotate around different roles within your business.

Under the umbrella of teamwork, every employee has the opportunity to develop new skills and grow in confidence.

Learning a new system challenges them and asks them to challenge themselves, while performance management keeps them on their toes. Nobody gets comfortable.

Making your team's life easier

HEY KNOW THEIR ROLE

The initial training they receive as the first part of your people development system, is comprehensive and consistent.

Ongoing, any updates to systems are communicated systematically, and training is always given for new procedures.

They feel ownership because they understand what they are doing, and are left to get on with it.

- They feel a responsibility to deliver for you and your customers.

THEY KNOW WHAT'S EXPECTED OF THEM

- They know that the customer comes first in your business, and are clear about the high standards that you expect.

- They understand how those standards and their performance in general is measured, and that there are both good and bad consequences relating to their performance.

- They get that they are responsible for their own development.

- There are never any surprises when it comes to their performance review as they receive regular, ongoing feedback.

THEY ARE PART OF A GREAT TEAM

- They know how their role fits into the bigger picture and that they are part of a well-drilled, high performing team.

- They feel valued as individuals.

- Everyone supports one another and can cover for each other because they have been taught all systems.

- The operation is smoothest when everything is working and they have enough resources and adequate supplies.

They know that you have a system for everything and that they will be fully trained and supported to learn.

They know the standards that you expect and that you are always looking to improve your systems as well as individual performance.

laking your customer's life easier

OUR CUSTOMERS KNOW WHAT TO EXPECT

Every transaction with every individual you employ is done in a regular and consistent way.

They don't have to think when dealing with your business, they know where to go, what to do, the standard to expect.

They feel comfortable dealing with you, and know that any changes that you make to policies or procedures or service delivery will be fully explained. They know you will support them through changes and this means less stress for them.

OUR CUSTOMERS GET CONSISTENCY

You do not have a high turnover of staff so your customers get to build relationships with your team and individuals within it.

They receive a consistent quality of service because all of your team have bought into your values and follow the same systems.

- Everything works as it should regardless of the time of the day or the day of the week.

- When you open up in a new geographic area, everything remains constant and consistent, except for the new faces.

YOUR CUSTOMERS ARE NEVER FACED WITH SILLY RULES AND POLICIES

- Your systems are designed with the customer in mind, and every employee has permission to question something that they feel is silly, or not helpful for the customer.

- From their orientation with your business, through their development and performance management, every employee understands that the customer comes first.

- Your team know that any calculated risks they take to satisfy their customers will be supported.

YOUR CUSTOMERS' EXPERIENCE IS PAINLESS

- There are no hoops they have to jump through.

- They do not have to repeat themselves to get what they want.

- Your service system and procedures are simple.

- You and your team are easy to do business with.

With so many benefits to be had, why would any business operate without systems and processes?

> *"Almost all quality improvement comes via simplification of... processes, and procedures."*

TOM PETERS

5 KEY POINTS TO REMEMBER

. A desire to make money does not make you a bad person.

. The most successful entrepreneurs have a greater passion for what they are giving their customers than for what they are getting in return.

. To grow your business successfully you need to know WHY you're in business.

. Invest time early in building the systems that will form your platform for growth.

. If you want to lose weight you have to get on the scales, and then set a target – it's the same in business. Where are you now, and where do you want to be?

f you do only one thing as a result of reading Part 1... Complete the Business Review which can be found t the back of this book.

PART TWO

Grow Your Business – Make More Money

"Disneyland is a work of love.
We didn't go into Disneyland just
with the idea of making money."

WALT DISNEY

CONSTRUCTING YOUR CUSTOMER EXPERIENCE

When the team at Bright look at a business, we look at it like an accountant would, focusing on revenue drivers (how we currently make money); and costs how we currently keep it or save it). What we're looking for is to see whether we're making £1, but spending £1.29 to make that £1.

Lots of people can make money, and lots of people can still go broke. The trick is in making £1.50 in the first place, by maximising your branded customer experience, and managing your costs to the point where, instead of spending £1.29 you're spending only 80 pence.

As I said earlier, there are only four key areas that you need to focus on in your business. On the Revenue side it's your service and *Branded Customer Experience*, and on your cost side it's your *People*, your *Operations*, and your *Financial Controls*. These are the only four areas that really impact growth, profitability and cash flow.

Many businesses don't realise that their whole operation runs on systems and processes, and those that do understand this, don't always appreciate how inefficiently their systems are running.

When you're looking to build your business, you have to start with your customers, who are they; are there enough of them; do they like you; and what do you have to offer them? This may sound like basic common sense but, as you probably know yourself, not every business has their customer at its centre.

Know your customers; find them, keep them, build long-term value-filled relationships with them and your business will grow.

Service is not a task, it is a state of mind.

Service is not a task, it is a state of mind. The how and the why, the mindset and the mechanics, whatever you want to call it, goes beyond the functional to building strong and lasting relationships. That said, like every other area of your business, there must be structure and process onto which can be built the 'magic'.

The companies who really get this were built around customer experience: companies like Virgin, Disney, Apple were founded on the belief that the customer's experience is everything, and they do what they need to do to make that experience not only the best it can be, but special.

Revenue won't build if costs aren't controlled effectively.

Your service won't work without efficient systems to support it, and great people to work the systems.

Bring these elements together and you'll find that not only do you have more time and more control of our business, but that you also have more profit nd better cash flow to fund your growth.

n Part 2 we will focus on your revenue drivers: our service system, and your branded customer xperience.

et's get started by looking at the basics.

START WITH THE BASICS

io back through the annals of time and you will nd that customers have always had the same five asic expectations. It's just that over the years, as ivilisation has progressed, from donkey, to horse, o car, to plane; and from stone tablet, to pen and aper, to computer, and back to tablet again, so ave our expectations.

Ve find ourselves in an age where everything must e smaller, faster, available, accessible, mobile, ortable, branded, and where 'must have now!' is he order of the day. And we have to keep up with he pace of change, not only living up to, but exeeding the expectations of our customers.

ietting the top five right is a good starting point for ny business.

1. Speed

"I feel the need... the need for speed."

GOOSE, *TOP GUN* 1986

It seems that nothing is fast enough these days. Time is such a valuable and limited resource yet, despite the increasing technological advances and time-saving gadgets, we all seem to be working harder and longer; glued to our Blackberrys and iPads, unable to escape from the hamster wheel of our working lives.

As customers we want what we want when we want it.

That may mean that speed is essential. We may decide that we are willing to pay a premium for guaranteed speed, and the smart company will ensure that they are prepared to deliver it for you. Think of the genius idea that is the Disney World queue-jumping, Fast Pass system, brainchild of someone who recognised that customers don't like queuing and would pay a premium for the privilege not to. Closer to home, we'll pay for faster broadband, next day delivery, direct planes and trains.

Immediate is the new fast.

t may mean that we want something on a guaranteed date. This is a much riskier prospect, and gain something for which we are often prepared o pay a premium. Florists, online gift shops and he likes of Moonpig, have made fortunes from this ustomer need.

)f course there are times when speed is a bad thing nobody wants to be rushed through a meal in a estaurant to free the table for the next sitting.

\nd other times when systems designed to make ervice faster for the customer actually slow things own. Have you ever used one of those self-service lls in the supermarket, and *not* had to call over the ssistant to help you at least once? Or is that just me?

here are certain times in our lives when we simply ave to steel ourselves for slowness:

Contacting any online call centre and having to wade through the treacle that is the automated system, only to be cut off at the final hurdle, or be greeted by an actual person, who then tells us that we should have called a different number.

Visiting a hospital A&E department – oh, the pain! Or any other hospital department where you have an appointment for a certain time, but still end up waiting for an hour or more, with little or no communication as to why you have been kept waiting.

- 'Popping in' to the post office on pension day.
- Going through the security checks at the airport.

We all have our personal dreads.

There are businesses who would previously have made it on to the list above, but have sorted out their act to the point that our previous expectation of slowness has been replaced by huge disappointment when they are delayed. I'm not sure that trains ever used to run on time – it was the rule that they were late – and now, it is certainly the exception, albeit still frustrating when they are.

The train companies have, by and large, changed our perception of their service, which is often significantly harder than changing the actual experience. But how have they done it, and what can we learn that will help us?

1. They recognised that there was a gap between customer expectation and experience.
2. They talked to their customers to determine the scope of the problem, and involve them in the development of a solution.
3. They invested in their infrastructure and equipment to ensure that technology did not let them down.

- They invested in their people, engaged with them, trained them and gave them better, more up to date information and systems to work with.

- They learned to communicate openly and honestly, for better or worse.

Ultimately, the key for each of us is to find a way to work to the speed that is desired, and expected, by our customers.

Managing a customer's expectations of speed is critical, not only to their positive experience but also to maintaining the integrity of your business.

> Managing a customer's expectations of speed is critical, not only to their positive experience but also to maintaining the integrity of your business.

If you expect your team to manage expectations, then give them a process to follow, explain the importance of following the process, catch them doing it right, and then reward them for it. It's that simple!

One of the best examples of managing expectations can be found at Disney where signs are installed for queuing customers (who haven't purchased their Fast Pass!) which tell them the approximate time left until they will reach the ride. Supermarkets use tickets at the fresh food counters to clarify a customer's position in the queue. Many call centres now use a timed 'countdown to answer'. Watch out for other creative examples, and steal ideas shamelessly!

A final word on speed. If you don't promise to be the fastest, then a quality service with clear time frames and managed expectations will win every time. But if you do promise to be the fastest, you had damn well better be!

2. A Painless Interaction

> **"Treat every small interaction with another person as an opportunity to make a positive impact in both your lives."**
>
> UNKNOWN

When you get into a black cab in London, you do so confident that your driver will be able to take you exactly where you want to go and by the quickest route. You're confident of this because every black cab driver has had to pass a special test, The Knowledge, before they can have their licence. It may be costly, but to you it's value for money, and makes your journey painless.

How wonderful would it be if every business went to such lengths to ensure that their customers had a painless experience. If we all made sure that our employees had all the information they needed, and that our systems were easy to do business with.

On the other hand, if you are always changing how you do things, or the layout of your website or store, or if you have a lengthy automated telephone system with a team who speak poor English at the end of it, you may have work to do to keep your customers.

As for knowledge, a customer's expectation varies greatly, depending on the type of business they are dealing with, and who in that business they are dealing with.

At the most basic level, for example, frontline staff in retail are expected to know:

- what their products are, and where products can be found
- what the special offers are and be able to recommend them to customers
- who the right person is to answer the customer's query if they are unable to
- the price and, where relevant, the basic functionality of products they are selling

If you're dealing with more specialist products, then a much greater level of expertise is required and expected. When you walk into the Apple shop, for example, you are confident that, like the black cab drivers, the Apple staff will get you where you need to go in terms of product type, processing power and portability.

What separates the best from the rest is knowledge combined with a real passion for the business and the brand. Talk to someone who is enthusiastic about their product and you cannot help but be engaged yourself.

> **What separates the best from the rest is knowledge combined with a real passion for the business and the brand.**

3. Friendliness and Respect

> **"Friendliness is contagious. The trouble is, many of us wait to catch it from someone else…"**
>
> DONALD ANDERSON LAIRD

People do business with people and most often with people they like. You'll hear that a lot in these pages. As customers, we would all rather deal with people who are friendly and approachable. It's an expectation, but it's not actually what we expect.

Of course, the worse the service around us, particularly from our competitors, the greater the opportunity to gain a competitive advantage as the exceptional business that breaks the rule.

The question you have to ask yourself right now is, 'How friendly is your business?'

How confident are you that your team are always friendly with your customers? Always welcoming and attentive? Always polite and respectful? If you're not sure, or suspect that they may not always be, then now is the time to turn things around and take advantage of this gap in the market.

Who we put in front of our customers, whether over the phone, face to face or on 'live chat', is hugely important, and can make all the difference in the world to our customer's willingness to do business with us.

Friendly, respectful service stands out. Our customers expect it, but get it so infrequently that it is always a pleasant surprise when they do.

. Availability

> ## "We can't plan life. All we can do is be available for it."
> LAURYN HILL

PEN ALL HOURS

In our 24-7 world, there is a growing belief that every business must be open and available every hour of every day. The web is worldwide, after all, and there is every chance that someone somewhere in the world will need us when we are asleep. Right?

Well, maybe!

In order to know if it's right for us, we must know for certain that it's what *our* customers want. And to be certain, we need to ask them.

Small fortunes have been wasted by companies who believed they knew what their customers wanted. Overseas call centres have been set up because they covered the night hours cost-effectively, but have lost both revenue and the custom of those who would rather speak to someone during daylight hours who knows the business and speaks the same language.

> **The only aspect of location that really matters is being somewhere that our customers can find us easily.**

Once we've asked our customers, *then* we can build our systems around their needs. And by now it will be no surprise to hear that we do need systems to ensure that we provide the consistency of service that every customer expects, whatever time they contact us.

I CAN'T SEE YOU!

Presence and visibility to our target market are key to business success. So, the only aspect of location that really matters, is being somewhere that our customers can find us easily. They don't want to, nor will they, spend hours searching for us. If we want their custom we will be easy to find, or they will simply go elsewhere.

In the days before digital, being 'easy to find' meant being a presence on every major high street and retail park. Ubiquity is still a key business strategy for the major players in retail, with McDonald's and Costa particularly adept at being available for their customers.

But even these big players have recognised the necessity of a web presence and, while they cannot provide their products online in the way of the pioneering Next Directory, they can connect with their customers, provide them with information about their business, and build a community.

Being 'easy to find' on the web is all about being on the first page of any Google search for the product or service you provide. This is where your customers expect to find you, and prospective customers won't even look anywhere else. Being there gets you found, and also says that you are a key player in your field, an expert, a source to be trusted.

A trusted business is also expected to be contactable by telephone, with numbers clearly displayed on your website. Our customers expect us to be available at the other end of a phone line, although, as we've said, they may not need, or want to call us at all hours.

EMPTY SHELVES

Of course, the availability that your customers expect is not just about whether or not they can find you, it's also about whether or not you have the product they want in stock. Regardless of whether you run a plumbing business, a bed shop, a restaurant, or an online bookshop, if you don't have the product or the part that a customer wants, when they want it, you may well lose their business, not just for this transaction, but forever.

It is such a gamble to minimise your stock levels, and it's very much a Catch 22: you don't think you will sell many of X so you don't stock them; a customer wants one, you don't have them, the customer goes elsewhere, you don't sell many.

Sometimes, in a small business you just have to take a risk. And the closer you are to your customers, the less of a risk it will be.

5. Value for Money

> **"Value is not made of money, but a tender balance of expectation and longing."**
> BARBARA KINGSOLVER

In the customer's mind, value for money will often be seen as the end product of delivering on all other expectations, and not as an expectation of a price.

If you are where your customers need you to be, if you have what they want when they want it, and serve them with friendliness and respect, they may not even consider the price to be important.

Yes, it's true that value for money means different things to different people, but it rarely means cheapest. And if you decide to go down that route, then you had better be the cheapest, as second place is nowhere in that particular race.

The value for the customer is in the relationship they have with you, in the quality of your product or service, in your willingness to listen and improve, in the consistency of your operation and their experience of it.

That is what your customers will judge you on.

So, they are the basics. Fulfil these five core expectations and you get to have customers, not a loyal following, but customers nonethe-

> **Value for money means different things to different people, but it rarely means cheapest.**

less. Against some of your competitors you may even stand out if you deliver all five well, but delivering a 'standard' experience will not make you special. You need a little more than that to be the brand that people tell their friends about.

> "Never be afraid to stand out. It's better to be remembered for standing out in a crowd than to be forgotten for blending in."

ASH SWEENEY

A STAND-OUT SERVICE SYSTEM

> "The only source of knowledge is experience."

ALBERT EINSTEIN

So, what is a branded customer experience?

Shaun Smith, the author of *Managing the Customer Experience*, would define it as 'the experience that becomes synonymous with your brand'; an experience that makes your customers love your brand, stay loyal to your business, and ultimately become advocates, telling all their friends and family about how great you are.

> An experience that makes your customers love your brand, stay loyal to your business, and ultimately become advocates.

We all have brands we love, they may be big like Apple or Virgin, but they can also be small like your local butcher or the Indian restaurant down the road.

And why do we love them? We love them because of how they make us feel, what we experience when we're around them, the emotions they arouse in us.

Maybe they 'invited us in', made us feel welcome like we belonged and very quickly made us feel part of a like-minded community.

Or maybe it's because they shared their story with us and made us feel like we were part of it. Think about Nike for a minute. Their story is not about making sports kit, their story is all about winning and reaching your goals.

Similarly, Harley Davidson's story is not about how they make motorbikes, it's about freedom, and reliving your youth.

For us at Bright, our story is not about coaching or consultancy, it's about liberation, about you having more time, more control and more profit.

That's the sort of story we want to build around you.

To create a Branded Customer Experience you need four elements:

. A great product that either solves your customer's problem, fulfils their desire or adds value in some other way to their life.

2. Efficient systems and processes that are easy to do business with, for both your customers and your people.
3. A team full of Brand Ambassadors – which means hiring people who share your values and *want* to serve customers; training them to work your systems; developing them as people; and both managing and rewarding their performance.
4. A great two-way communication system with your customers and your team that proactively seeks feedback and listens to it.

When you build your branded customer experience, you build great relationships with both your customers and your team, and a loyal following of brand advocates who bore their family and friends about how good you are.

Truly loyal customers can't imagine doing business with anyone else.

First Impressions last

The initial impressions of our business will be different from customer to customer. For some it may be a flyer posted through their door; for others it will be our website or our Facebook page; for a different group it will be face-to-face, hearing us pitch at a conference or networking event. Whatever way potential customers learn of us, that first impression has to be a good one, the message has to be lear and the presentation professional, representing ow we want them to view us going forward.

hink about a business you know that made a big irst impression on you and set the opinions you still ave of them today. What made that business stand ut for you, for good or bad, and do you still feel ositively or negatively about them based on those iitial thoughts?

or me, the standout is Virgin.

Vhat a big impression they made on me with their ed branding and their slightly self-mocking com- nunications and adverts an impression of a very ifferent brand that was emented on my first ong-haul flight when ichard Branson walked own the plane thanking veryone for flying his irline. 'Different', 'fun', ustomer-focused' are the vords that I associated

> **Every experience starts with that first impression and, based on that alone, some people will choose not to be our customers.**

vith Virgin from those first impressions, and they ave stayed with me ever since.

very experience starts with that first impression nd, based on that alone, some people will choose ot to be our customers and go elsewhere. Those who like us, or who choose to give us a chance, will learn more about us as they journey through our systems, interact with our people, maybe visit our premises, and they will have thoughts and feelings which either confirm or dispel their initial opinion of us.

For their experience to enhance our reputation, every step of their journey with us needs to fulfil their basic expectations and also give them what they want specifically from us. And, of course, it must solve their problem.

THE IDENTIFICATION PROCESS

Who are your customers and what do they want to experience from you?

How often have you heard business owners saying, 'Well, my customers are everyone really', or, 'I deal with any business that uses computers', or 'My target market is any business with up to 500 employees'? You may even have said something similar yourself and if you have done so recently, you are still taking aim with a blunderbuss and will never truly hit your mark.

If you haven't already done this, it is worth figuring out who your ideal customer is by asking yourself questions like these:

Who is he/she?

Where do they live? What sort of home?

What type of company do they have, or what business do they work in?

What is their disposable income per annum?

What type of person are they?

What do they do outside work?

Have they spent money on your type of product/ service before?

How successful are they?

What car do they drive?

What papers/magazines do they read?

Knowing who your ideal customer is makes it so much easier to talk to them and get their attention.

As a business with designs on growth and profitbility, the further we are able to drill down to our niche market, the more successful we will be in giving them a great customer experience.

Getting on the Right Track

What would you say the difference is between customer experience and customer service?

There are various definitions of both, but for me, Customer Service is a person-to-person interaction either over the phone or face to face, while Customer Experience is the sum of all of the customer's interactions, thoughts and feelings about our business or brand from when they first learn of our existence: their first impression of us and their emotions and reactions to all the various touchpoints during their journey through our business to the last.

> **Your customer track is the end-to-end experience of your business, through the customer's eyes**

This is your customer track. The end-to-end experience of your business through the customer's eyes.

It is something that you should map out, know intimately and keep up to speed with, because it will change as sure as society, trends and fashions change.

Even the most basic process mapping exercise will help you to understand:

- where and what all of your touchpoints are
- who in your business provides the service at each of them
- what the customer's reaction is, including their emotional response at each point

Understand these fundamentals, know where your hotspots are, and you have a foundation on which to build a great experience.

Customer journey mapping is one area where you really should sweat the small stuff. As customers ourselves, we know that little things really matter:

econds shaved off a service time, a smile on a bad day, a helpful word of advice, a please, a thank you.

To carry out an effective mapping exercise you really need to understand who your customers are, intimately, and be able to put yourself into their mind to understand their thought process and their emotions as they move from point to point along your customer experience.

You have to be able to remove yourself from the vendor track – or your version of events – completely, in order to see, feel and think like your customer, and not be limited by your existing operating process.

If you're in business for the right reasons then your intuition about your customers has a great chance of being correct.

As you work along the customer track, note your thought process, the decision points, what works for you, what puts you off, what blocks your progress, who the people are that you interact with, what their strengths and weaknesses are, what you would like to see or experience that is currently missing.

Trust your gut when it comes to this exercise. If you're in business for the right reasons – the ones we discussed in Part 1 – then your intuition about your customers has a great chance of being correct. Believe what you feel and then engage your team to build an experience around your brand that you and they would want as customers.

Staying on track

You'll have heard the old adage, 'If you're not supporting the customer, you are supporting someone who is'. Having a team who understand this is crucial to delivery of your branded customer experience. You simply can't afford to have individuals who feel removed from the customer and don't understand their impact or how their role fits into the bigger picture.

Think of your marketing: whoever does it for you, they will often create that first impression for your prospective customers. How well they deliver your message; how well they connect with those prospects on an intellectual and emotional level; how friendly they make you sound may determine whether your prospects do business with you. Do they promise something you can't deliver or do they represent your brand in a way that has your existing customers nodding in agreement?

If you outsource your marketing, how can you make sure that they 'get' your business well enough to communicate its heart, as well as its products, to your customers? What access will you give them to our team, to your customers, to your ideal customer, that will give them the information they need to make this vital first contact for you? You are putting the first touchpoint of your customer experience in their hands; how have you ensured that it is in good hands?

And what about those who do your billing? What process are they working to? Do your customers get accurate invoices, laid out clearly; are they sent out on time and not chased early; do your suppliers and associates get paid on time? Do they speak directly to your customers to sort out any issues and, if so, what tone do they use?

Customers talk, suppliers have friends and family. Those who deal with invoices are very much involved in your customer experience.

Everyone in your team has a role to play: we need to help them see how all the pieces fit and understand their role in creating a consistently positive and painless experience.

Wacky Races or Formula One?

In Formula One, every team member is drilled to perfection, they know their role and how their role fits into the overall operation. They know that they have a key part to play and that any slip-up affects the whole team – and they rarely slip up.

In Wacky Races on the other hand, everyone is out for themselves, they are only concerned with their own race and, while they are still heading to the same finishing line, far from being helpful and supportive, they will go out of their way to hinder one another and be disruptive.

Where does your team sit right now on the Wacky Races to Formula One scale?

Wacky Races   **Formula One**

If you're already at Formula One, there may not be much in this book that will improve you further, but if you're tending the other way, please read on.

> "Get closer than ever to your customers. So close, in fact, that you tell them what they need well before they realise it themselves."
>
> STEVE JOBS

GROW YOUR RELATIONSHIPS

The customer experience is made up of a series of relationships.

An old boss of mine once famously said to me, 'It's not about relationships, Marianne, it's about results,' and I have spent the intervening years happily proving her wrong. If you want to grow your business – and even if you don't – it is *all* about relationships, with your customers, with your team, with your suppliers, with your bank manager. Relationships deliver results.

Grow your relationships with your customers

We work People to People and, in the final analysis, people do business with people they like.

First they get to *know* you – through your marketing, through referrals, through your employees, through face-to-face meetings with you. They get to know what you do, the quality of your products and services, the sort of people you employ, the values you have. And they start to build a picture of you based on that very first impression from that very first encounter.

> **It is all about relationships. Relationships deliver results.**

Then they make up their mind whether they *like* you or not. Maybe they share your values, they like how you build relationships, your products and services meet their needs really well, or perhaps they just connected with you as a person. Based on the simple fact that they like you, they will then do business with you.

At this point you haven't quite gained their *trust*. They don't know you well enough yet, have not had enough experience with you to make that move from liking to trusting, but you can build that trust over time by consistently getting things right for them and solving their problems.

I don't know if you have come across the idea of a Trustbank before, but it's a metaphor that works well for me. The idea is that the customer has a Trustbank, and every time you perform well, and live up to your brand promise, a deposit is placed in the Trustbank and your account grows and grows over time.

If you make a mistake or perform badly, you make a withdrawal from your account, but if the account is healthy, your relationship will survive. If, however, you make mistakes early on in the relationship, or a major error at any point, the goodwill in your Trust-bank account will become overdrawn and your relationship will be in serious danger of total collapse.

There are classic examples of trust being destroyed completely through one act or one major problem from which there was no coming back. Two from relatively recent history are Gerald Ratner's pronouncement that the jewellery he sold in his shops was 'crap'; the other was in 1982 when Pan Am Flight 759 crashed, killing over 150 people. Both were successful companies at the time, but neither was able to recover the trust of their customers and both failed soon after these incidents.

Trust is huge in any relationship. Being trusted can make the difference between getting by as a business and being really successful.

One of the most powerful benefits is being referred by customers who know your work, like you and trust you enough to recommend you to their friends and colleagues. It's one of the best ways to build your business and can save you a small fortune in marketing costs.

Create Customer Advocates you know, the people who sing your praises and tell others about you, who love

> **Trust is huge in any relationship.**

you and your brand and the way you do business, and want the world and his wife to know how good you are – and you will probably never have to advertise again.

I'm an advocate of a small production and event management company called FourImpact, who have built their relationship with me and earned my trust over a number of years. They are such a great, reliable, fun team to work with. They are always busy; they never advertise, they simply look after their customers, keep them, and get lots of referrals. There's a lesson in there for all of us.

I'm pretty sure you feel the same way about a brand you use. I think everybody does.

Whichever way you look at it, and whatever terms you use to describe it, your customers' relationship with you, and the sum of all of their experiences with you and your team, will determine how successful your business will be.

Become a mind reader

Back in the days when I had a PA, one of the questions I always asked at their interview was, 'Can you read minds?' It was very important to me that I worked with someone who could do that – anticipate my needs, be one step ahead of me, understand the way I wanted to work and get there before me – and you would be amazed at how many good PAs can do just that, and how valuable they are.

We need to read our customers' minds, anticipate their needs and do just a little bit more than just what is expected of us. Any old business can do that satisfy their customers. But how many focus on delight? On surprising their customers with something personal like a card on their birthday, or on their first anniversary as a customer, or to say thank you for a big order? On special awards for being the 100th customer today/this week/this month? On throwing in a little something extra just because…? Some businesses do, but not many.

Just like a good PA, you have to put in the time and effort to get to know your customers well enough to read their minds. You have to work at knowing, and remembering, the small details of your customers' lives like birthdays and anniversaries, and hobbies and favourite sports teams. And then you have to work at doing something with that information.

Knowing the particular problem that your business resolves for the customer should be a given, but staying up to speed with how they're doing will mean picking up the phone, arranging a meeting, taking them for coffee or lunch, dropping them an email – any of which will show that you care for more than just the money they paid you, and make them feel that little bit special and looked after.

Learning to think like your customer is the most obvious next step, and falls into two categories:

1. **Thinking like a dissatisfied customer.**
   Asking yourself…

   - What has really cheesed you off as a customer in the last month?
   - Is there anything in your list that could apply to your customers?
   - What would your customers say are the top three problems for them?
   - How can you eliminate them?
   - What is the first step?

2. **Thinking like a satisfied customer.**
   Asking yourself…

   - What great expectations did you have as a customer last month?
   - Is there anything on your list that could apply to your customers?
   - What would your customers say are the top three things you do for them?
   - What can you do to build on them?
   - What is the first step?

Working through this exercise either on your own or, better still, with your team, on a monthly basis, could provide you with a wealth of information and insights and take you one step closer to mind reading.

Your team need to see you acting in this way, going to this amount of effort to improve small details for our customers. Talk is cheap. It is what you do that's important and that will encourage behaviour that matches your own.

> **Talk is cheap. It is what you do that is important and that will encourage behaviour that matches your own.**

go-to people

As customers when we do business with a company, we often seek out certain individuals because we trust them. They are our 'go-to' people, and we are confident that they will give us the right information, help us to choose the right product, and ensure that we get value for our money.

In an information world, where Google and others like them give our customers immediate, but often competing, answers to their questions, the real power of knowledge lies in being that trusted source. I'm pretty sure that as you're reading this you can think of your trusted sources for financial or marketing advice, choosing the best laptop, the right outfit, the best holiday destination.

In the retail world, that trusted source is often John Lewis; in the world of public transport it might be the Trainline; for financial matters, the Martin Lewis website.

Who is the trusted source in your industry or market? Is it you and your business?

My go-to people all have a positive attitude that makes it a pleasure to see them, or talk to them on the phone, or even chat to them online. They all smile, they all have a friendly, helpful way about them and they make me feel special. Their body language, where I can see it, is open and they give me their undivided attention, apologising if they are distracted or interrupted by a colleague. They always try to make things easier for me, explaining anything I don't understand in a clear and non-patronising way, and they will tell me if their product or service is not right for me, which makes me trust them more.

My go-to people are good with all customers, and patient with those who are rude and aggressive. They also seem to have great relationships with their colleagues and appear to enjoy their work. They are the sort of people I want working with me.

So where do we find these people, and how can we become a 'go-to' business?

Well we start by being extremely choosy about who we hire, only hiring those with a great attitude:

- to work
- to life
- to customers

People who share our values and the values we want to instil throughout our business.

Ve train them, we give them the skills, the informa-
ion and the support they need to serve our custom-
rs with confidence. And
hen we reward them and
hank them every time we
atch them building rela-
ionships with our custom-
rs and making their day.
Ve'll talk more about this
n Part 3.

> **Go-to people are priceless and the more we have, the more our business will be viewed as a go-to business.**

n a P2P (people to people)
usiness, go-to people are priceless and the more we
ave, the more our business will be viewed as a go-
o business.

isk Taking

Jot everybody enjoys risk, and it's even harder to
eel easy about encouraging your team to take even
alculated risks to add value to a customer. But
ome businesses do it, and reap the rewards of
mpowered employees delighting their customers.

Iyatt Hotels have a mission to provide what it calls
authentic hospitality', defined – in the words of
EO Mark Hoplamazian – as 'making a difference
n the lives of the people we touch, including guests,
mployees and others.'

s part of a new effort to take better care of its Gold
assport members, the company targets those guests

with pleasant surprises designed to delight them during their stay, empowering hotel employees to perform what they call 'random acts of generosity'.

Hoplamazian wrote in a blog post, 'Don't be surprised if Gold Passport picks up your bar tab, comps your massage or treats your family to breakfast. It's part of bringing authentic hospitality to life and making you feel more than welcome.'

A similar example comes from Wings, a credit card brand owned by one of Turkey's largest banks, which partnered with five upscale restaurants in Istanbul to offer a random selection of lucky cardholders a pleasant surprise. After having dinner at one of the restaurants and paying with their Wings card, the customer was notified that Wings would foot the bill.

Reward the random acts of added value from your team; catch them doing things right, even the smallest of things, and recognise team members, publicly, for their actions. Every day, and every time you do this, you strengthen the customer culture of your business and build the relationship between your people and your customers.

Grow your relationships with your people

We've talked a lot about our external customers and how we can best serve them, but we mustn't ever forget that our people are our customers too, and if we want them to be go-tos and risk takers, we have to show them the same level of respect and support.

Of course we probably believe that we do this already, that if we have the right values we naturally treat our people well, and hopefully that's true. But what would our people say?

If you gave your team the following 10 statements, and gave them the answer options 'Always', 'Sometimes', 'Rarely', and 'Never', how would they answer them?

1. _____ (your name) says 'Good Morning' to me when I arrive for work.

2. _____ is positive and consistent (not moody) day to day.

3. _____ says 'Well done' when I've added value to a customer.

4. _____ looks for opportunities to praise the team.

5. _____ uses mistakes as learning opportunities for the team.

6. _____ keeps us informed and up to date with how the business is performing.

7. _____ asks my opinion and listens to suggestions for improvement to service.

8. _____ knows my name and pronounces it correctly.

9. _____ thanks me every day for a job well done.

10. I trust that _____ wants me to be the best I can be.

How do you think you would do?

Are there a few there that might get rated 'sometimes' or 'rarely'?

> **Your Employer Brand is just as important as the brand you market to your customers.**

Hopefully there are none that would be rated 'never', but if there are, now is the time to start doing something about them.

Your Employer Brand is just as important as the brand you market to your customers, since it's your people who either do, or don't, live up to your brand promise.

What is your reputation as an employer? What promise do you make to your employees? What do you think your employees say about you and your business when they're out with friends?

If you haven't really thought of it before, what do you want your employer brand to be and how can you make it so?

We'll talk more about strengthening your reputation as an employer later; suffice to say that there are huge benefits to be had from having employees and ex-employees as advocates of your business.

Grow your relationships with your suppliers

So far we've talked about loving your customers. We've said that it's equally important to love your employees, but there's one other group that is essential for the stability of your business: your suppliers and associates.

The people who you do business with in support of your customers are often every bit as vital to your success as your own team – sometimes more so, and yet we can't always say that we treat them well, can we?

If we were to work through a similar exercise to the one we have just completed for our team, how would our suppliers rate us?

Would they say that we have an excellent partnership?

That we always treat them fairly and communicate honestly and directly?

That we look for win-win agreements and contracts?

And what about invoicing? Do we quibble over pennies on every invoice, or do we pay on time and in full?

What is our reputation with our suppliers and associates? Do they work with us because it's a great experience, or do they put up with our treatment of them because they need the money?

Are they complaining about us at parties, or telling other business friends that we're a great bunch to work with: firm, but fair and friendly?

If we're treating this group differently to our customers and our people, what are the consequences? What message does it send to anyone who observes this behaviour?

The Supermarkets (and I generalise) have a very bad reputation for the way they treat their suppliers, often backing them into win-lose situations and forcing them to cut their margins to non-sustainable levels. The fact that I know this means that their suppliers talk – to other suppliers, to friends, to the papers. It also means that I avoid the supermarkets that I know do this and go to one that I believe to be more ethical. Yes, I may be forced to use them on occasion, but my choice now would always be to avoid them, and I cannot be alone in this.

> **We're in the People 2 People business, and all relationships matter.**

People do business with people they like and trust – both customers and suppliers – and people want to work for people they like and trust. Who wouldn't?

We're in the People 2 People business, and all relationships matter.

THE PROCESS OF COMMUNICATION

When we have a good relationship with our customers, when we know them intimately, our message to them immediately becomes clearer.

We are able to talk to them as we would to an individual, perhaps to a friend.

We can connect with them at an emotional level and, over time, build levels of rapport which ensure that they know us, like us, and trust us.

We can sell the benefits of our product or service to them because we know the problems that they have and how we will solve them.

There is no customer alive who doesn't want to know what's in it for them.

How we will help them

What we will give them

What the value is to them

What guarantees we offer

What really matters to them? It's probably not what we think!

"In business you get what you want by giving other people what they want."

ALICE FOOTE MACDOUGALL

Ultimately, most customers want us to solve a problem for them. If you think about a classic house-cleaning advert, they always begin by showing you the filthy sink, bath or floor, and only then do they show you the product that will clean all of this mess up for you with little effort on your part and in a jiffy.

"Flash cleans floors fast – and no messing!"

We need to know what our customer's problems are, to have a PhD in the things that block their route to growth, to peace of mind, to control of their business.

If we focus on those, if we tell them how we will solve their problem, there is a chance that they will want to connect with us and become our customer.

It is only when we know who our customers are, and have a great product aimed at solving their problems, that we should begin to focus on how we will deliver our message.

Treat every communication as individual

The best way to communicate with an individual is to personalise the message to them as far as possible, so that it reads as if they are the only person we are communicating with. Even when they know that they are not, this is still impactful.

A couple of big tips:

. Don't be dull; use appropriate humour if you can, and
. Do it differently to everyone else.

Standing out from the crowd: fun ideas for personalised communication

Hand delivered helium balloon with postcard

Cat with a 4ft tail for selling office space: 'If you can't swing this cat...'

Valentine's card or Easter card

Unusual business card

Different coloured envelopes

Teabag: 'Make a cuppa and have a read of this'

CDs and DVDs

Lumpy mail, eg a bar of chocolate, a cuddly frog, by courier

Mocked up newspaper in a frame featuring the individual using your product

---

Choosing the right communication system

Many of us think 'internet first'. We rely heavily on our website and social media, and ignore more direct ways of contacting customers like mail shots and the telephone, based on either the perception, or the reality, of the costs involved.

But it's worth noting that reported sales from telephone and postal communications are consistently excellent, and that using the postal service when so few others now are (due to the increased costs), not only makes our correspondence stand out in a much smaller crowd, but also satisfies the occasional need to communicate with those who have never embraced the digital world.

However we choose to communicate our messages to our customers, we should be systematic about it. As a minimum we need a process for:

- storing and updating customer data
- keeping communications regular and relevant
- measuring and monitoring the success of each

Let's take a look at a few of the key communication systems and tools, and a few top tips for how you can make them work better for you.

YOUR WEBSITE

A website really is a must have communication system in this day and age. Even those customers who like to touch and feel products before they buy them will still expect the business to have an online presence.

We've all been there, seen a product in a shop, liked it, and gone online to see if we can find it cheaper. It's an expectation. In fact, many of us are annoyed if a business has a website, but no online ordering process, which means we have to call them up to place our order.

There are websites and websites, however. As we said earlier, if your website is not set up properly, it might as well not exist because few will find you, and those that do will bounce off your page as soon as they arrive on it. It's not just a case of looking good, although that is important – we all know about the importance of being on page 1 of Google, but how many of us have the first clue about how to get our business there?

And just to make it more difficult, Google change and update their criteria fairly regularly, although it must be said that it is usually in favour of the likes of us, who simply want to do straightforward and honest business with our customers, and who don't have time to cheat the system.

There are several elements which remain constant in the Google criteria, which are listed below. Take a few minutes to check out the Google-friendliness of your website against these eight essentials:

Website Essentials

Professional design and branding
Your website must look good and your brand logo and colours must be appropriate for your target market. Google likes Wordpress websites, so this is an ideal platform on which to build your website. It's also easy to manage yourself.

Opt-ins'/data capture mechanism

A successful business has an effective database of interested prospects and existing customers. Your database needs to have a means of capturing names and e-mail addresses, and a great way to get that information is to offer something in exchange.

Video

Google now owns YouTube, and they love video on a website. It doesn't have to be professionally shot, and it doesn't have to be very long, but it does need to be there!

Clear Message

How clear and clutter-free is your home page? Is it immediately obvious to anyone who might chance upon your website, what it is exactly that you do? Is it punchy enough, with text broken up by pictures and videos? How powerful is your pitch?

Call to action

Linked back to the data capture, do you ask your customer to act in some way? Buy now! Claim your free guide here! Join our club today! This type of call to action works, so don't shy away from using it.

Social Media Links

As we'll talk about shortly, social media presence is not only expected by web-savvy customers, it's also a great way to build business when you know what you're doing.

Proof

Social proof, particularly in the form of video testimonials, is extremely powerful in persuading customers to buy from you or work with you. So, if you don't have any on your website, grab your flip camera and go video a few of your customers saying great things about you.

Contact Numbers

Even if your website is very clear and easy to do business with, there should always be a contact number for those customers who would rather do business over the phone, have a question, or wish to give you some feedback. Top right hand corner is the ideal, but wherever your number is, it should be clearly visible.

HOW DID YOU DO?

Really well, hopefully – maybe because you have employed specialist help to keep this particular plate spinning. If you didn't do so well, help is at hand in the resource section at the back of the book.

Knowing what to include in your website content, and how to display it to maximum effect, is the foundation of online success, and if you don't know, or don't care enough about this, then you need to be working with someone who does. It really is that important.

SOCIAL MEDIA

There appear to be two camps when it comes to social media: those who love it and are very active, and those who hate it, but recognise that it is an essential element in their customer communication armoury.

There is an immediacy with Twitter and Facebook that you don't get with other forms of communication and, when you know what you are doing, they can connect you to a group of customers you might not otherwise have reached and increase your sales dramatically. Thanks to the amount of personal information that people give about themselves on these sites, it is also possible to be very specific with your communication.

A couple of examples:

1. A speaker at an event I attended told the tale of how he had been visiting Durham to make a presentation and had tweeted that he was there, using the hashtag #Durham. A local deli owner, who had set up his Twitter account to monitor anyone who was visiting Durham, tweeted to the presenter that it would be great if he visited the deli while he was in the area. So of course he did, and was given such a great experience that he has been back there several times since, and taken others there both virtually and physically.

2. A direct marketing business owner was looking to offer supplementary income to people who would be able to deliver a leaflet campaign for him. Thanks to Facebook, he was able to advertise specifically to postmen in the Rochdale area,

aged 30-35. In doing so he saved time and money for his business, and ensured that the campaign had a better chance of a successful outcome for his customer.

ocial Media tools are powerful but, as with your vebsite, if you are not systematic about using them, hey will be a drain on your time and serve you no urpose. If possible, you should look to delegate his activity or outsource it to a specialist company. 'd be happy to recommend one to you.

n the meantime here is a suggested...

30-minute social media routine

witter

Follow someone every day
Add someone to a list – follow@listwatcher
Tweet an article from your blog archive
Re-tweet two tweets and add a comment – schedule via a programme like Hootsuite or Tweetdeck
Tweet a visual

acebook

From your business profile, 'like' at least one other business
From your personal profile, comment, like or share at least one item
Share an image

- Tag @someone in a post, eg I saw @John Smith at...
- Pose a monthly question – use poll survey and ask your friends to vote
- If relevant and appropriate, check birthdays and comment

LinkedIn – business page
- Add a poll discussion and tweet it (duration two weeks)
- Add one person from 'people you may know'
- Share your business profile with your network
- Ask for recommendations for your business
- Be active on a group discussion
- Blog (weekly)
- Write an article
- Upload to a networking site eg Google+, LinkedIn Groups etc
- Post on Facebook, Twitter, Linked in via Hootsuite's RSS atom which sends to all
- Post to article directories to index it and register on Google's radar
- Comment on another blog or business forum eg UK Business Forum

Other (occasional)
- Add a book review to Amazon, Good reads and LinkedIn
- Register a new alert on Google alerts

EWSLETTERS

A printed newsletter is one of the most effective ways of building a long-term relationship with your customers and, although it may take 6-12 months before it starts to pay off, it is well worth the wait.

There are six key benefits of the printed newsletter over other forms of communication, including the e-newsletter:

- Builds a community of your customers. A newsletter is seen as a publication rather than advertising and will build trust and a relationship with your customers.
- Increases your credibility and positions you as an expert in your industry. People pay more to do business with an expert.
- Creates an opportunity to showcase customer successes, to highlight referrals and thank customers for them, and to increase your sales by doing both.
- Gives you the opportunity to give something back to good customers by giving them exposure.
- Has greater longevity. A printed newsletter, delivered through your customer's door, will almost certainly not be thrown straight in the bin and, unlike an e-mail, cannot be deleted. These things hang around.
- Helps to build your brand through all of the above.

Print is still most people's preferred way to consume large amounts of information, and it doesn't have to be glossy and expensive.

It's a people thing

And yet even now, with so much technology available, the best and most effective way to engage with our customers is face-to-face. We all know the importance of a good first impression, a firm handshake, a clean and tidy work environment, a sense of order, building rapport with excellent eye contact and a warm smile. Those are things that have stayed with us since school.

Ultimately, people want to do business with people they like – yes, we also need to be able to scratch their itch, remove their pain, resolve their problem – but that first impression, coupled with how we pitch our business in those first few vital minutes, will determine whether or not we are going to get the opportunity to talk further.

So how's your pitch?

I'm lucky to have learned the art of pitching from one of the very best in the business: the man who pitched for First Direct and Egg, before turning them into billion pound businesses, Mike Harris.

What Mike would say is to build your pitch around the following four questions, and then deliver it with passion and enthusiasm.

What's your idea, expressed clearly and without any ambiguity?

Where's your credibility, why should I listen to you?

What problem are you solving that is relevant to the person you are talking to?

What do you actually do to solve the problem?

Simples!

There is huge value for both you and your customer if you get this right. You have the opportunity to build a long-term relationship, and they get to have their pain removed by someone who knows what they're talking about. It's a win-win outcome.

It's an unfortunate truth that we can often lose sight of our customer in the fog of how we will communicate with them. We spend days, weeks, months developing our websites, our Facebook pages and our Twitter profile, and precious little time working out the basics, like who our customers are, what we want to tell them, what their problems are and why on earth they would pay for our products and services.

It we want to hit the mark with our communication systems and have them drive our business success, then we need to spend more time on the identification process and have a robust and meaningful customer feedback process.

Of course, we don't always get it right for everybody and, if you remember that those who have a problem with us will tell ten people more than our advocates, we had better make damn sure that we look after them, nurture them and, if possible, turn them into advocates!

It's a customer's job to complain; we all do it, and not always that well either (it's still not a very British thing), and our customers' initial reaction to a face-to-face meeting might well be to trot out all of the things that are wrong with the way we do business, or have done business with them. Great. Welcome the feedback. It is a gift, and should be recognised as such.

We want to improve our business, after all, and our customers are in the best place to tell us how, so we listen, respond positively,

> **Welcome feedback. It is a gift.**

and then, back at base, rather than using it as a stick to beat people with, we work out how we can use it to make our business better.

YOUR CUSTOMER FEEDBACK SYSTEM

Obtaining and utilising customer feedback can often be a frighteningly complex and onerous process, but it's a vital element of your customer communication system and, if handled effectively, one that will have the biggest positive impact on your business.

The following five-step process has always served me well.

STEP 1. ESTABLISH WHAT INFORMATION YOU WANT AND HOW YOU WANT IT

Once you've made the decision to seek customer feedback proactively, the first step is to decide what information you want, what areas you want to focus on, and what aspects of service you want to understand better.

Think about what your customers have told you so far and consider starting in those areas.

For example, they may have talked to you about your speed of service; how easy it is to use your service; your delivery; how often they have recommended or referred you.

Once you've decided where you want to focus, your next step should be to consider what sort of information you need to know. For example, do you merely want to know if something isn't working, or do you want to know *why* it isn't?

Are you going to ask closed (yes/no) questions which will give you limited information, or open (who, what, where, when, why, how) questions, which will give you much more detailed information, but perhaps more than you need.

Or, you may choose to use statement questions (eg, 'I am always satisfied with the speed of service'), and a sliding scale (1-10, Strongly agree-strongly disagree).

Being specific both with your questions and your response mechanism will provide a robust platform for constructive feedback and the identification of any trends.

STEP 2. WHERE ON THE CUSTOMER TRACK?

Many businesses make the mistake of thinking that customer feedback is something you look for once the transaction is completed. While it's true that post-service feedback is potentially a wonderful insight into your end-to-end customer experience, there are a number points along the customer track that present equally valuable opportunities for feedback.

Potential Customers

Google Analytics provide you with a powerful insight into your website visitors, what pages they looked at, at what point any conversion to sales took place and, most importantly, at what point the potential customer left your site. Such detail and trends can help you to understand what's working well for your potential customers and what needs to work differently or better.

Some websites use pop-up questionnaires as a potential customer leaves the site. The most effective of these ask a few quick and easy questions with tick box responses that simply aim to understand why the visit hasn't converted to a sale.

During the Customer Journey

Some time ago, I read about how National Express survey their customers via text during the journey, giving them the chance to leave in-the-moment feedback. This approach is now being employed by several other companies – including Eurostar, who also utilise this open line of communication to keep their customers informed of travel news relating to their journey.

As the transaction is completed

Several e-commerce websites have feedback mechanisms built into the point of transaction. Without even realising it, customers are providing feedback to these sites as an integral part of their journey from virtual basket to virtual payment. The options are usually few and simple, needing only one or two quick clicks to complete.

Other sites ask for feedback as part of their Thank you or Next steps message to customers, again with a flawless integration that makes it feel a natural part of the customer journey.

After Completing the Transaction

Companies such as Sky and Orange frequently send a text survey immediately after telephone calls to capture their customer experience. Others, such as eBay or Amazon, ask that you rate your experience over a range of experience areas (eg price of delivery, quality of item, etc).

Capturing customer feedback post-transaction is the default position for most providers; possibly because it presents an immediate snapshot of a customer's end-to-end experience. However, by limiting yourself to the end of the journey, you're potentially missing out on valuable detail and information. Your customers are human and their end-of-the-process feelings and overall experience will inevitably replace their in-the-moment feelings and experiences.

Positioning your feedback mechanism at a point where the experience remains fresh and real for your customer will provide you with a truly valuable insight into their most instinctive thoughts and feelings about the experience.

STEP 3. DECIDE ON YOUR METHOD OF CAPTURE

Seeking customer feedback has never been so supported or undemanding. It used to be that capturing and analysing customer feedback was an onerous or

omplex process. Now there are any number of
products available that can be used at any point in
our customer experience and can make the process
s involved or as automated as you want.

Whatever survey mechanism you choose:

Keep it short
Keep it relevant
Keep it convenient

Many successful businesses have recognised that
customer opinion will exist with or without them
and have positioned themselves in the most visible
arena to manage it – social networking sites.

We've all seen the social media pages – 'I love this
business', 'I hate that business', 'the other business
never delivers on time'. Proactively setting out your
tall in the middle of all this, by creating your own
business page, gives your customers the opportunity to give you their feedback about you.

Equally importantly, you have the chance to manage and respond to that feedback as it is raised –
giving you the very real opportunity to strengthen
public perception of your integrity and raise your
public profile.

There is no such thing as a right or wrong way to
gather customer feedback, but there will be one or
more ways that are right for your customers and

your business. As no one knows your business like you do, only you can decide.

STEP 4. USE IT OR LOSE IT

One of the biggest errors we can make is to leave a big gap between collecting feedback and acting on it. There's a delicate balance here: move too quickly and you may miss the true trend; move too slowly and, by the time you've resolved the problem, your customer may well have moved on.

One of the most critical things to understand is what you're going to get from your results before you start, understanding the format of your results, how you'll analyse them, what they'll tell you and why.

Investing your time to get this right, up front before you begin, will ensure that your response can be swift as well as informed.

STEP 5. EVERYTHING IN MODERATION

Sometimes businesses are so keen to gather feedback that they ask their customers to complete a survey that resembles the Domesday Book. Others have a relentless pop-up box on their website that just won't go away. Don't swamp your customers with requests for feedback, or you could end up with none.

Whether it's by pen and paper or expensive software, it's vital that you consider customer feedback as an investment in the growth and sustainability of your business. The risk of not doing so is that everyone other than you knows the customer-facing weaknesses of your business.

Taking feedback positively, having a system to collect it, to analyse it, to action it, sends a strong signal to your team that customer feedback is a good thing. Yes, there may well be the odd customer who tries it on, but don't treat them as the norm and make them your excuse for not acting on the legitimate criticism.

There will also be people who just disagree with the way your business operates – a difference of opinion that you may simply want to acknowledge, note, and file but not discard. You never know when a pattern of this criticism may grow to the point where you really need to take action.

Listening to those customers who are less vocal, and who don't offer feedback of any sort, is also important. We should never forget them, or assume that their silence means they're happy. Remember we're British, and everything is always ok until the waiter is out of earshot!

Don't accept the 'F' word either. 'Fine' is not good, or great or excellent. Fine is often, 'actually I'm really not happy with your customer service, but I don't think you're worth giving feedback to, so I'll just not do business with you anymore, and tell all of my friends that you're rubbish.' 'Fine' is a scary word and always demands further enquiry.

First-hand feedback is priceless, and the fact that you show yourself to be open to it demonstrates your desire to be better than you are.

> **"The two words 'information' and 'communication' are often used interchangeably, but they signify quite different things. Information is giving out; communication is getting through."**
> SYDNEY J. HARRIS

PEOPLE + PROCESS = A GREAT CUSTOMER EXPERIENCE

The truth is, even the warmest, most polite, most smiley people can be a block to our customer satisfaction if they are not given good systems to work with and fully trained in how to use them.

Customers want consistency in their dealings with us; they don't want to have to explain what they need several times to several different people before they get it. They want a quick, painless interaction with someone who has clearly been trained to a good standard, and has enough knowledge to be of real help.

We can all rub along fairly well without systems, but only while we have a small team who were there at the start, and know not only how everything works, but also the standard we expect of them.

The minute we bring in additional people to cope with additional business, both

> **The only way to prevent potential chaos is by developing and documenting systems and procedures that the whole team follow.**

the knowledge of 'the way things work', and the standards, are diluted, as they are passed from existing to new employees. In a matter of months we have a situation where everyone is dealing with customers in their own way, and to the standard they *believe* is expected; turning what was close to a formula One operation into something more akin to Wacky Races.

How quickly do you think you start to ship customers when that happens?

The only way to prevent this potential chaos is by developing and documenting systems and procedures that the whole team follow.

From a purely financial point of view, having a system for your service is essential for ensuring that you don't miss opportunities and leave money on the table. Great staff are an excellent starting point, and your customers will respond to their politeness and friendliness, but are you really making effective use of these people you are paying (hopefully) good money for?

If not, you could be limiting your revenue, and ultimately your ability to grow.

By way of example, the other day, I met someone for a meeting in the bar area of a restaurant. We met at midday and ordered coffee. Over two hours later, we both remarked that we had sat in front of a menu offering 'lite bites and lunches' for the entire time and yet, although the place had been well staffed, no one had come near us to ask if we would like something to eat.

Why was that? Was it that they thought they would be intruding? Did they think we might shout at them to go away? Did they assume that if we had wanted something we would have asked? Who knows? Maybe it just didn't cross their mind.

For the business owner, what that meant, over the course of a two hour lunch period where the bar was pretty full, was a whole heap of lost potential sales. It's true that people don't always say yes when asked, but if only 20% of that full bar of people said yes to food, or a second drink, the staff wages would have been paid for those two hours at least. That's money left on the table.

And all for the lack of a system.

There was no question about the friendliness of the staff. They were great. They just weren't expected to upsell; it hadn't been built into their role and wasn't a standard part of the process. That's money left on the table.

The trouble with not making effective use of your resources is that it severely restricts your revenue and, ultimately, your ability to grow. Sadly, most businesses don't even realise that they have this problem, probably because it is much harder to spot something that's missing, than something you are doing badly or incorrectly.

In many cases, what is *not* being done is upselling.

Whether subtle, or unsubtle, upselling can be hugely effective if done well. For example, suggesting that a jacket goes with a particular pair of trousers, or that for £5 per month you could have access to certain exclusive information about your new purchase online, or perhaps that 'you might just fancy one of our lovely fresh croissants that have just come out of the oven, with your coffee'.

Upselling is not just about making more money (although that is always a benefit), it can also be a means of giving a customer added value and greater choice, for example in bundled deals and packages.

What opportunities are you missing in your business?

How could you be making more cost effective use of your most valuable resource: your people?

Where could you be making more money?

5 KEY POINTS TO REMEMBER

1. A great customer experience is built around logical systems and customer-focused people.

2. Customers have 5 basic expectations which must be satisfied.

3. It's all about relationships. Relationships deliver results.

4. Build an experience around your brand that both they and you would want as customers.

5. People do business with people they like and trust.

If you do only one thing as a result of reading Part 2...
Map your customer's journey through your business.

PART THREE

Grow Your Business — Save Money

"To put it bluntly, I seem to have a whole superstructure with no foundation. But I'm working on the foundation."

MARILYN MONROE

A COST-EFFICIENT OPERATION

As we said at the beginning of Part 1, lots of people can make money and lots of people can still go broke. Maximising your revenue is only one half of the growth equation, the other is control of your costs and managing them to ensure that you achieve a profit on every sale.

Your ability to control the costs around your *People* your *Operations* and your *Financial* controls will have a real and significant impact on your business growth, profitability and cash flow.

Your whole operation runs on systems and processes, and they need to be running efficiently.

Revenue won't build if costs aren't controlled effectively.

Your service won't work without efficient systems to support it, and great people to work the systems.

Bring these elements together and you'll find that not only do you have more time and more control of your business, but you also have more profit and better cash flow to fund your growth.

In Part 2 we focused on your revenue drivers: your service system, and your branded customer experience.

In Part 3 we're going to zoom in on your two major areas of cost, your people and your operation, and see if we can't improve the productivity of your team and the efficiency of your operating systems.

YOUR OPERATING PROCESS

If you think about sport, any sport, game day/race day/fight day, is just the culmination of weeks, months or, in the case of the London 2012 Olympics, even years, of preparation. There may only be a elect few out there performing, but there are often hundreds behind the scenes who have helped to make that performance the best it can be.

Formula One racing is a great example of this. Only one man drives the car, but what a team he has around him to make sure that both he and the car are at their peak for every race. The driver may get to stand on the podium and have his picture taken, but in Formula One they win or lose as a team.

> We all have processes in our business. We may know them simply as 'the way we do things around here'.

This is exactly what it's like in business. There will only be one person who talks to the customer either face to face or over the phone, but whether they win or lose with that customer is dependent on the rest of the team, the quality of their resources, and the effectiveness of the business processes and systems.

Whether we recognise them as such or not, we all have processes in our business. We may know them simply as 'the way we do things around here'.

They are rarely 'designed' at the outset, often because small businesses usually begin as a one-man band. At that stage, you're just getting on and doing things in what seems to be the most logical way. As you add people, they tweak your process to make it work better for them; as you add technology your process changes again to make use of it; and as your business grows, your process evolves into 'the way we do things around here'.

There's never been any time to examine whether it's the most efficient way, whether we are wasting money or wasting time, whether it's the best way for our customers. We're simply too busy doing the doing to find out. It's a common scenario, and one that stunts, if not completely kills business growth.

Often we add IT into the process, to save time. Maybe we chose a programme that was recommended; we've done our research online, and other business owners are speaking well of it. We added a CRM, because you 'have to have one' as you grow. And a third system because what we have still isn't quite doing everything we need it to. None of the systems talk to each other; we have to make lots of manual interventions and enter the same information several different times into each different system.

So we decide bespoke must be the way to go – our business needs are unique, after all, and the software developer has said they can pull something together that will answer all of our prayers for under £50k. But, oh dear, between the testing of the

ew system and keeping on top of the developers
nd the bugs that keep appearing we decide to write
hat off too, and just go back to the Excel spread-
heets we started with. We can always just add a
ew more columns, after all.

ound familiar in any way?

etting IT right

T can be very costly, so before we launch into buy-
ng it we need to be very clear about what exactly
ve want it to deliver, how it will support our opera-
ion – and if we really need it at all.

'o achieve this clarity, the first thing we will do is
nap out the way we currently operate: the sequence
f events that take us from the start of our operation
ɔ the end. There are several ways to do this, all
vith academic sounding names like value stream
nalysis and the DMAIC process, but one, my fa-
ourite, is often simply called 'the brown paper
xercise', which, as the name suggests, requires a
arge roll of brown paper along with coloured post-
t notes and big fat marker pens.

ots of fun, and very useful too!

'he idea of the brown paper exercise is to show you
he big picture: the forest and the trees of how the
ɔrocess works today (not how it *should* be working);
vho is involved; what actions or activities are per-

formed; and to highlight where there are delays; where there is duplication or waste; where an activity is adding value to the customer and where it is not. It tells the story of your operation, warts and all, in a very clear and very visual way.

In order for it to work effectively, you need representation from three groups of people:

1. Those involved in the operation, to tell it how it is, and to make suggestions for how it could be.

2. Someone independent of your team to view things from the customer's perspective, to look at where you could cut service times, where you could add in proactive communication, what hoops you are making the customer jump through.

3. An individual I like to call 'the child': someone whose role is to ask 'why?' as often as necessary, to root out the 'because we've always done it this way' elements in your process.

When you complete this exercise with all the right people involved, you will discover a whole host of opportunities for making your processes more effective. The sort of weaknesses that it will highlight include:

- Dead zones – places where work sits, gets held up (a bottleneck), or gets lost

- Lost time – where people have to go looking for work
- Checkers checking the checkers – too many approval layers
- Duplication of work
- Broken interfaces (could be technical, or a personality clash between two of the team)
- Value-added vs non-value-added activities (ie, value to the customer)
- Specific outcomes of a role in the process
- Physical distance travelled to complete certain tasks (eg, from one floor to another)

To achieve buy-in for any changes needed, it's important that your team are tasked with pulling together a report detailing all the issues that were highlighted and possible solutions to the problems. They should also be asked to make recommendations both for immediate action and for the long term, with continuous improvement in mind.

See the 'Need More Help?' section at the back of the book for more information on how to do this exercise.

In doing your brown paper exercise, you may well call into question your existing IT and you may feel that you need a system that supports your team and your business more effectively. Before you leap in to buying something new, I'd like to suggest that you think about the following:

- Your situation is unlikely to be unique. There will always be someone who has had the same needs as you, and has put in the time and spent the money on research and development to create a solution. You do not want to go down the bespoke route and have to deal with all the snags, bugs and glitches that new programmes inevitably suffer.

- Do your research or, if all of this is just a minefield for you, invest in someone to do it for you.

- Look for 'open source' products which are more likely to have plug-ins and allow links to other software.

- Investigate the full capabilities of the systems you have; you may find either that they are not robust enough for the long-term, or that they have more capability and capacity than you think, and you don't need to buy another system.

IT systems are there to support rather than replace your process. They can add tremendous value in terms of cost savings, but if the wrong choices are made they can also be like a pit, swallowing up your precious resources of time and money.

> People who have no time to do it right, but always the time to put it right spend 10 times more money dealing with their failures than they would in prevention.

Investing time in reviewing and adjusting your operating process may seem a costly exercise, but there's a well-known statistic that says that people who have no time to *do it right*, but always the time to *put it right*, spend 10 times more money dealing with their failures than they would in prevention.

"Successful people ask better questions, and as a result, they get better answers."

ANTHONY ROBBINS

YOUR DAILY ROUTINES

Business Set Up

A Place For Everything, and everything in its place! Key to the success of your operating system will be ensuring that your people have the resources they need, when and where they need them. Having things to hand, and always putting them back where they belong, will make everyone more effective and make the experience smoother for your customers.

If you were a plumber, for example, you'd have a place in your van for every tool that you use, and at the end of the day you'd make sure that every tool was cleaned down and put back where it belonged. Not being this organised and not investing time in making sure that your set up is right, will not only waste precious time when dealing with a customer, but can also give the customer a very poor impression of your work standards and customer care.

I saw a great example of this recently at one of the large prestigious retail stores. They had had a major refurbishment and, as part of this, they had either chosen to remove the 'wrapping area' from behind the counter, or had forgotten to build it into the new plan. False economy or bad planning, either way, what it meant for the staff was that they either had to go through to another department to wrap a customer's purchase in tissue paper, or wrap it up on the floor in the space behind the counter! The staff I witnessed had chosen the latter option, perhaps to save time, but it looked awful, and was not what you'd expect from this particular retailer.

You may have heard of 'blind organisation', where staff know where everything that they will need lives, and are so confident that it will be where it should be that they can find it with their eyes closed. This is the level of organisation you should want for your business, as it not only makes your

eam more productive, but it also makes the cus-
omer experience that much more enjoyable.

MOMENTS OF TRUTH

arlier we talked about customer journey mapping,
nd the importance of knowing and understanding
he customer's experience of every interaction you
ave with them, from marketing right through to after
ales service. Part of that mapping process will be to
pot the Moments of Truth, and to work out a way to
ither deal with them or eliminate them completely.

Moments of Truth are those key moments in the
ustomer's interaction with you that have the poten-
ial to make or break the relationship. They do not
lways show themselves to you as key moments,
ut for the customer, they can be the difference that
nakes the difference.

or example, a potential customer may be undecided
who to use to get some work done, and have nar-
owed their choice down to you and a close competi-
or. They've checked out your websites (you both
ave one of a similar standard) and that hasn't
elped them, so they decide to call: this is the first
noment of truth for them. How long will the call
ake to be answered? Will it be answered by a person
r by a machine? Will they be friendly and helpful?
What will they say to differentiate themselves from
heir competitor, either positively or negatively?

Based on how you have set up for business – what systems you have in place to ensure that your customer's call is answered promptly, by a friendly, knowledgeable person who not only wants to, but can help them you will either win or lose their custom.

The level of empowerment you have instilled in your people, their willingness to take risks to satisfy a customer, their confidence, will also be a crucial factor for those unexpected Moments of Truth: an unusual request from a customer, perhaps, or the breakdown of a piece of equipment.

Build a team around you who understand and know their roles, and give them a strong foundation of systems for every area of your day-to-day business, and they will not falter when it comes to those Moments of Truth – not even the unexpected ones.

DANGER ZONES AND HOT SPOTS

Very closely linked to Moments of Truth are those permanent Danger Zones that are a key part of the customer experience and cannot be eliminated from your system. In many instances, these will be related to your promotion and advertising: what you have promised versus how you deliver.

In a restaurant situation, it might be the difference between the quality of food you have promoted in words and pictures, and the actual food that the customer receives. For a mobile telecom company, it may be the promise of a consistently good signal, and what the customer experiences. In both cases, you may only get the one shot at winning their long-term business: one visit in the case of the restaurant; one contract in the case of the mobile phone company.

This is where it's useful to have your systems backed up and verified by someone outside your team. A restaurant owner has no choice in the matter, they have external verification thrust upon them by the powers that be to ensure the safety and health of the general public. But every business would benefit from having a fresh pair of eyes test their systems through a programme of quality checks, systems audits and, where appropriate, mystery callers or shoppers.

We are often too close to our operation to see its flaws and, while some of our customers may be very vocal when they are disappointed or unhappy, most will just walk away and find someone else to give their custom to.

A third, more objective pair of eyes is what is required to ensure that the way we work continues to meet our customers' needs. These spot checks don't have to cost the earth either; they can be done by a family member or as a quid pro quo with a business colleague, and could pay dividends if they spot a gap in your operation through which you are haemorrhaging customers. Of course, you would have to listen to what was being said and not come up with a million reasons 'why we do things this way', but if you can swallow your pride, you will continue to improve your operation.

2. The Travel Path

A basic but essential process in any business owner's toolbox is the travel path. If you have not come across this concept before, the travel path walks you along the customer's journey through your business to check that everything is as it should be for your customer. It is hugely effective for retail businesses, but it is just as important and useful for businesses which do not, as a rule, have face-to-face interaction with their customers.

In order to make it effective, your travel path will be completed with a checklist in hand which details the customer priority areas and the essential elements that should be in place for each area. Alongside each requirement will be a box to confirm that it is either up to standard, or not.

Ideally your travel path will be completed by you or a manager at the start of every day, and then at set intervals during the day if you feel it would be of benefit. It doesn't have to take long, maybe just 10 or 15 minutes, but it is a good investment of time for you or your team leader.

By the time you have completed your travel path you will know that your team are all present and in place; that they have the resources they need to serve your customers; that all your equipment, including phone, fax, server, is up and running; that the work area/customer areas are clean and well organised; that your staff have fresh coffee or water available; that the toilet is clean and stocked – in other words, the full picture of how your business is set up to operate for the day. If there are things that are not right, you'll complete your travel path, and then put together a prioritised list of actions you need to take.

Like any other area of your business, it is important that you see the whole picture rather than tackling the first issue that you come across when there may be a bigger priority just around the corner. It's also important that you make a note of any issues that have the potential to develop into trends, particularly those relating to your people.

. Targets and Motivation

How much fun do you have in your business? Do your staff come into work every day looking forward to working with you? Do you do your bit to help them enjoy what they are doing, even on tough days?

As the leader, you set the tone and the mood of your organisation day-to-day and week in, week out. Your enthusiasm and positive attitude will rub off on your people and make it ok to be light-hearted and to have a bit of banter. And if you've developed a professional team they will know the fine line between letting off a bit of steam, and not focusing on their work.

Setting targets for your team (or better still, having your team set their own) on a regular basis can make a real difference to the direction and momentum of the day, and be the difference between outstanding and mediocre performance.

Small change, big difference

Understandably, business owners worry that they are going to have to make wholesale changes in order to impact their growth, profitability and cash flow, but the truth is, it is often just a small tweak here and there that will begin to turn things around.

It may be physically moving a piece of kit that is slowing down or blocking your service; it might be moving a team member to a role that is best suited to their skills; or perhaps it could be having you work at the coal face once a month to get a feel for your customer experience.

> **Often just a small tweak here and there will make a big difference.**

Going back a few years, Starbucks used to take payment for their coffee, after you had finished drinking

t. They lost a lot of money this way, with around 0% of customers walking out of the door without paying. Yet it wasn't until someone sat down and did the numbers, and mapped the customer track, that they realised why their revenue was not what it should be. Armed with this knowledge, they made the one small change – moving the payment step forward to just after you order – that made a very big difference to their worldwide revenue.

What is the small change in your operation that might just make a huge difference?

"There can be economy only where there is efficiency."

BENJAMIN DISRAELI

A HIGH PERFORMING TEAM

We established earlier that you're passionate about what you do and that you have a real desire to have everything in your business done to your exacting high standards. We also established that you can't do everything yourself, there simply aren't enough hours in the day and, even if there were, if you want to grow your business, you have to get it to a point where you can take yourself entirely out of the day-to-day and feel comfortable to delegate and follow up on the great team you work with.

It's not enough to have great people. If they aren't clear about their role or what they are expected to do, they will end up like the guys in Wacky Races – everyone going in roughly the same direction but in their own way and at their own speed. The sort of business that wastes a lot of money.

What we want is a well drilled, high performing team with everyone knowing what their job is, how to do it and doing it really well. And also knowing how their role fits into the bigger picture. The sort of business that uses funds efficiently and effectively.

So how do we achieve these consistently high performance levels?

We hire people who really want to do the job; we train them in our processes and systems, then we practise over and over and over again. We correct and coach individuals when they make a mistake, we celebrate when they perform well. It is a whole team effort; we win or we lose, as a team.

Where did your team sit on the Wacky Races to Formula One scale?

Do you have team players with a great attitude working for you?

Do you have structured processes and systems which keep everything in your operation running smoothly and consistently?

Do you develop your team and manage their performance to keep them on track?

A high performing team is not a nice thing to have, it is an essential business requirement that will make you more money, and help you to save it too.

THE HIRING PROCESS

How to hire the right people

The first thing you need to decide is whether to hire at all. Could you buy the skill elsewhere? A virtual assistant, an accountant, a sales team are just some of the skills that you can pay for without hiring an individual. Most business owners these days take this option one way or another while they are growing.

Once you've made your decision to hire, the next question is 'money-maker' or 'business support'? In the early stages of many businesses, the individual you will hire will need to be both. But as you grow, the ratio between these two groups has to be very carefully managed and will be based on the needs of the business. Too many support staff and you will be wasting money as they won't have enough to do. Too few and your money-makers will be burned out trying to grow revenue and deal with their own admin. It's a fine line that can either make or break a business. And it's only one of the many considerations when hiring new staff.

No matter how much we might want to be, we can't be everywhere all of the time. Sometimes we just have to rely on and trust others. A scary thought? Well, maybe, but less scary if you only hire people who share your values and who will love your customers and your business, almost as much as you do.

> People who share your values and who will love your customers are the right people.

People who share your values and who will love your customers are the *right* people, yet how many businesses even consider that to be possible, let alone an option for them? Hiring individuals for their ability to relate well with others, for being positive, for having a happy smile? It really doesn't seem to be high up on the agenda for many, and all too often individuals are hired for their polished CV, for the fact that they have a good degree, or two more GCSEs than the other candidates.

Our priorities have been skewed towards those who have achieved a certain intellectual standard, and we often overlook those who are bright as a button, full of life and determined to do something with their lives. By today's standards, my dad, who left school when he was 14 and definitely falls into the latter category, would have been rejected as a no-hoper and yet he, like many similar 'no-hopers', went on to build his own very successful business.

Sometimes we have to be able to spot a diamond in the rough, and if we truly want to have our customers loved, we have to go for the people who have a great attitude, a positive outlook on life, who enjoy people, who want to learn, who want to serve – and reject everyone else, no matter what.

Think about a standout service experience you have had recently and jot down the answers to these five questions.

1. What were the personal qualities of the individual who served you?
2. What made them special?
3. What about their appearance? How did they look?
4. How did they interact with you?
5. How did they make you feel?

When I was growing up, and being teenagerish about doing my homework, my mother used to threaten me with Woolworths: 'If you don't knuckle down, you'll end up working at Woolies,' she used to say, implying that my standards would never be high enough for Woolies' polar opposite (in her world at least), John Lewis.

My mother initially had a similar view of McDonald's, the 'glorified fish and chip shop' with which I enjoyed a very successful career, so she may have been prone to making judgements based on her own perceptions – but the point is that most of us do. Most of us decide who to give our business to based on who we interact with, and with all due respect to anyone who was associated with Woolworths, it is no real surprise to anyone that they are now out of business while the John Lewis Partnership flourishes.

The benefits of hiring the right individuals are there for all to see. How many people tell you that when they have an expensive item to purchase they'll get it from John Lewis because they trust them? And what is that trust based on? Thousands upon thousands of individual interactions between customers and John Lewis staff that have been handled so well that those customers have talked to friends about them, written blogs about them, recommended that their family go there and, of course, they have gone back themselves.

Other organisations have got this sorted too, and stand out as a result: Apple and their knowledgeable and helpful staff; First Direct Bank, who will go out of their way to provide 'heroic service' day and night; Virgin, who always look to make things easier, and fun, for their customers. These organisations have the right people in the right places who love their customers, and, guess what? Their customers love them right back!

These are the sort of qualities that you want in your people and it's important that you settle for nothing less, because the consequences in terms of damage to your repeat business, to your reputation – both as a business and an employer – and to your overall success, could be of Woolies proportions.

Where to find them

The first piece of good news for us, if not for those who are unemployed at the moment, is that it is a buyer's market. There are loads of really good people who have taken redundancy, either willingly or unwillingly, or who have left school or university and been unable to find a job that matches their talents and qualities.

The second piece of good news is that the 2012 Olympics changed the British perception of British service and made it cool to be great at it. We get that we are a service rather than a manufacturing country now, and it's ok to enjoy serving customers.

And the final piece of good news is that these people are everywhere. There are great people working in businesses which don't love their customers today, who would jump at the chance to join you if you sell the role well.

What do they look like?

In the same way as we asked you to create your ideal customer, it's important that you also create your ideal employee. Make yourself be specific about the demographic you would choose: the age range, the situation they're in, whether they're married or single, just left school or just fancied a change. You can't hire to these ideal demographics (for a start it's not legal), and there is a great deal to be said for diversity within a team, but simply going through the exercise will focus your mind on the pros and cons of different demographic types.

A woman with children, for example, may be limited in terms of her hours, but may have skills that you don't need every hour of the day, and may also be an excellent mentor for someone who has joined you straight from school.

A school-leaver or graduate may have dreams and ambitions way beyond the role you offer, but could benefit from the work and life skills offered while they save.

An individual recovering from redundancy may benefit from the confidence boost of working for you, and have skills and experience that you could benefit from in return.

What's your ideal? Someone with a great attitude who wants to learn and develop? Someone who enjoys the challenge of winning over a difficult customer? Someone who challenges you because they don't think that your business is customer-focused enough? What are their personal values? What are their reasons for working? What do *they* want to be known for?

Think of the Team

When thinking about the individual that you are looking for, it's always a good idea to keep in mind the make-up of your team. Whether you already have a small team, or know that you will need one, it's a good investment of your time to think now about 'money-maker' or 'business support', as we've already said, but also about the strengths and qualities that will help your team to gel.

You may decide that you want individuals who are creative. Great! But leading a team full of amazingly creative people that is not balanced with a few practical 'doers' may be like herding cats. Similarly, if you have a bunch of detail people and no big picture thinkers, you could get bogged down for weeks without achieving anything! There has to be a balance: chiefs and indians; thinkers and doers; creatives and completer-finishers.

The same goes for skills. There may be work that you are doing now that you want to pass to your new employee. Do they have the skills or can they be

> **We are looking for those who are good at building relationships and who naturally achieve rapport.**

trained, for example, in book-keeping, website and social media management, call handling?

If you're looking to build a team, then those who already enjoy team sports would be a good place to start, and may also provide you with possible leaders for the future. Most importantly, we are looking for those who are good at building relationships and who naturally achieve rapport. These people will not only be good with your customers but will almost certainly be good teammates also.

How to hook them

So now we're ahead of the game: we know what our ideal employee looks like, sounds like, acts like and works like. We know the role this individual will fit into within our business, and that we are hiring their personal qualities and values as well as their skills. We know they will have the X factor we are looking for.

Let's go get 'em.

The advert

Unless you are able to headhunt all your favourite go-to people from the businesses you use, you will need to start with an advert, like the rest of us.

Your advert is going to set the tone for everything that follows so, if you intend to have a fun working relationship with this person (and it should be written as if it is just to one person), then your advert should, at the very least, hint at a sense of humour. 'Superstar required: no super powers necessary, just...'

It should be honest about what the job is, and what it is not, and it should showcase what you offer to your employee that will benefit them way beyond their salary.

You want this advert to stand out from the crowd, so how about throwing out a challenge to your prospective employee. Rather than them sending you through a CV, which will tell you everything you need to know about their qualifications, but nothing you need to know about their qualities, their values or their attitude to customers; ask them to prepare a five-minute video of themselves explaining 'Why you and your customers will love me'. This will be more fun for you and them, and almost certainly make the shortlisting process easier!

THE INTERVIEW

Your interview process could follow the standard format of 20-minute interviews over the course of a day or two, depending on the number of applicants, or, as you're looking for that X factor, you could try an *X Factor*-style interview process.

X factor hiring was first introduced to me by a marketing guy called Nigel Botterill, and I love it for its creativity, its focus on attitude and diligence, and its speed.

How it works

- Filter your initial applicants down to a maximum of 15
- Invite them all to take part in the 'selection process' at 7.30 am (or the time that you would need them to start work) and give them only limited information about where to come. This tests both their commitment to getting the role, their punctuality and also their ability to find out where they are meant to be in order to get there on time.
- At 7.31am, close the doors – anyone who arrives after this time, regardless of their excuse or reason, is thanked for coming, and sent home.
- Take the photo of those remaining and give them a name badge and coffee
- Line the candidates against the wall
- The decision-maker (you) then comes in and welcomes everyone, and explains that while this

is a different selection process to what they may be used to, by 9.30am, someone in the room will have a new job.

- Each of the candidates in turn is then asked to tell you something about your business. Nothing too difficult, this is just to check that they have made the effort to do a little internet research about you and your business. You don't need someone who can't be bothered to find out the most basic details about you, so those who are unable to answer their question are thanked for coming and asked to leave.

- The remaining candidates are then broken into teams to complete an exercise, such as: a space-craft has crash-landed on the moon, you have salvaged 15 items, put them in order of priority. The exercise should take no more than 10 minutes and is just to get them comfortable and for you watch them interacting.

- Once the exercise is completed, the candidates are asked to sit in the circle of chairs that have been arranged for them. The interviewing team (ideally the same number as the candidates) will then carry out speed interviewing, rotating around the circle spending five minutes with each candidate, asking them each a pre-arranged question, eg.
  - Best boss you ever had, and why?
  - What's the big plan?

- o How do you prioritise your work?
- o What's your proudest achievement?
- o Why should I hire you?

- It is important that the interviewers are well-drilled and that they focus fully on the person in front of them at each point.

- The candidates are then sent for a coffee while the interviewing team review what they have learned about each of them. The photographs are very important at this point, acting as a memory-jogger for those who cannot easily remember names. This process will often throw up a very clear winner with the team, but just to be certain from a business perspective, two are taken through to final interview.

- All candidates are told what is happening, and those who have been unsuccessful are thanked warmly for applying and taking part in the interview process, before they are asked to leave.

- The final two candidates are then interviewed formally (and separately) by the panel to determine which of the two will be chosen to join your team.

- Choose and hire!

By the time you have awarded the position to the chosen one, you will have saved yourself at least half a day over the usual formal interview process, and almost certainly be more confident that you have the right person for your team.

Try it for yourself.

YOUR INVOLVEMENT

How close you stay to the hiring process will determine how successful you are in building a team of people who share your values and love your customers. Yes, of course you might make mistakes; who hasn't misjudged someone at some point in their lives? You have a much better chance, though, of getting it right first time if you make hiring a key priority.

Stay involved at every step. If you're not personally writing the ad, make sure that you check the content, the grammar, the spelling. Make time to check the shortlisted applications and, if you haven't done the rejecting, to spot-check the discard pile. Be present at the interviews and play a full part.

If you follow the X *factor* method, we are only talking half a day of your time – but what a valuable half day! You get to show your people how committed you are to the team, you get to ensure that you hire the right person for your team and the business, and you show the individual how important you believe that they are.

If this is your first employee, you need to set the initial benchmark and not let that quality slip when hiring additional team members. You know your ideal person; now you need to determine the standards and values you want to instil within the team.

THE RULES OF THE GAME

What are the Rules of the Game that you want your team to work to? The values and standards that you expect of them? The commitments that you make to each other about the way you work together? Communicating these at the point of hiring leaves an individual with a clear picture of the sort of team they are joining and the behaviours that are required of them.

Your Rules of the Game could include the following:

- Our Mission – what's the purpose of your company, your reason for existing?
  - o 'Our mission: to inspire and nurture the human spirit – one person, one cup and one neighbourhood at a time.' (Starbucks)
- Our Values
  - o Whatever is most important to you: honesty and integrity, strong customer relationships, development of your people – you decide. These values should be those that you personally live by.
- Our Customer Ground Rules
  - o How you want your team to work with your customers.
- Our Team Ground Rules
  - o How you want your team to work with each other.

- Our Rules for Risk-Taking
  - When you will and when you won't support risk-taking on behalf of your customers.
- Our Team Behaviours
  - Different to team rules, in that these are individual responsibilities, eg towards personal development, taking feedback positively, how you communicate – in writing or verbally.
- Our Management Team Behaviours
  - Your commitments to your team, eg to communicate openly, to be honest, to respect their opinions.
- Our Management Team Communication
  - How you will communicate with the team, and how regularly you will communicate.
- Being Professional
  - What professionalism means to you, and how you want the whole team to demonstrate professionalism.

If you have an existing team, this is a great exercise to involve them in; it tells you what is important to them, and shows them what is important to you. Once completed, these Rules of the Game become commitments from one team member to another, from you to the team, and from all of you to the customer.

Before you begin any hiring process, it's a great idea to revisit your Rules, along with the profile of your ideal employee, as a reminder to you, and anyone else you are involving in the process, who *precisely* you are looking for. This will then set the tone for the advert, for the interviews and for the orientation of the new person. It will also create the foundations for your employer brand.

See the 'Need More Help?' section for bonus 'Rules of the Game' template.

"Hiring the Best is your most important task."
STEVE JOBS

PEOPLE DEVELOPMENT

As we've mentioned before, your reputation as an employer, your employer brand, is as important as your business reputation. It should be a key part of what you want to be known for:

- **Developing** – good team players, leaders, managers, young people; helping every individual achieve potential.
- **Having fun** – working hard, playing hard; an enjoyable place to work; great team spirit.
- **Caring** – supportive, flexible, understanding.
- **Fairness** – everyone treated fairly.

The benefits of a great reputation as an employer show up both on the bottom line and in the workplace. Your customers notice how engaged your people are; you have a very low turnover of staff; your hiring costs are

The benefits of a great reputation as an employer show up both on the bottom line and in the workplace.

minimal; your re-training costs are low. Your people talk about how much they enjoy their work to their friends, their family, out at the pub.

They feel tremendous loyalty to you and your business, not only while they are working for you, but long after they have left you and moved on. This word of mouth acknowledgement of how good you are as an employer, this tremendous loyalty, is a powerful force and of great benefit to you as a business.

Ask companies like Miele, McDonald's, John Lewis, Apple how they have benefited from looking after and developing their people, and they will tell you that it is priceless.

Ask ex-employees of these companies what they gained from their time there, and they will talk about how they were developed, the opportunities that opened up for them, the fantastic team spirit and work ethic. Some may talk about the financial benefits, but others pay more and do not inspire this type of loyalty.

First Impressions

Your reputation as an employer will begin when a prospective employee first sees your advert.

While they may have known you as a customer, formed opinions of you, your team and your business based on their interactions, and may even have thought how great it would be to work for you, they will only begin to form their personal opinions of you as an employer when they see your advert and apply for your vacant position.

This is when the time that you spent on the advert will prove its worth. If written well, your ideal employee will read it as if it is written directly to them, will get that your business is a good fit for their values, their team spirit and their work ethic, and will be keen to complete their application and get to interview. Their first impression will be a good one if the ad is well written, professional and fun. It will be even better if they receive a response by the date stated on the advert.

For those who will *not* make it to interview, it is very important from a reputation standpoint, not to mention common courtesy, that you let the individuals know that they have been unsuccessful. I don't care how many applications a business receives, if someone has made the effort to apply for a job, they deserve to hear from you that they have been unsuccessful, and not be left hanging round waiting for a response that never comes. It's just bad business.

Regardless of how you decide to do your interviews, your employee's first impression of you will be dispelled or confirmed by their first-hand first experience of you.

- Does their interview start at the scheduled time?
- Did you greet them personally and introduce them to the rest of the team?
- Were you on time, and looking appropriately smart?
- Was the whole experience professional yet relaxed and supportive?
- How respectful were you of those who were interviewed, but were not successful (as these people will also take away an opinion of your employer brand that will be shared with others)?

The old cliché that you never get a second chance to make a first impression is so very true. And with an employee who you expect so much from, it is vital that you get the tone, the warmth and the professionalism right from the very first meeting.

First Day

Do you remember your first day at work, how nervous you were, how anxious to make a good impression? For a new employee it is a very big deal, and yet many organisations are horribly complacent, casual and slapdash about it, not only failing to make it a big deal, but failing to be prepared at all. How many stories have you heard about employees turning up for their first day only to find that they aren't expected; that the person who does the orientations has not shown up, and they have to sit round for hours waiting for someone to see to them; that the whole thing is just a total shambles?

I've certainly heard enough (and experienced one such first day myself) to know that it leaves you feeling very flat as an employee, wondering if you've made a mistake, wondering if this is really the organisation that you thought it was.

You don't want this to be how your new employee feels on their first day. You want them to go home buzzing, inspired, excited about getting started with you – don't you?

So, get the day planned, make sure that the rest of the team know when their new team mate is arriving, what their name is, and what you have planned for them. Make sure that you have everything

ready, and make it spe-
cial – for every new em-
ployee that you hire.

Don't ever get tired of
making a first day a spe-
cial day for your business.

Don't ever get tired of making a first day a special day for your business.

Orientation

Opinions differ regarding when a new employee should be oriented into, or shown the ropes of the business. Some people like to do it on the first day and get it over with, but for me, the first day should be a welcome to our team day ; an introduction to the people with a brief overview of who does what, and where your new employee fits into the bigger picture.

The Orientation, can then take place on the following day, when the new employee is more focused and less overwhelmed by the newness of everything.

As the orientation is key to the new employee's success with your business, I would always recommend that you are present to lead the three key elements, which include:

- More detailed information about the different aspects of your business
- An introduction to the buddy system (if you have one), and their new buddy

- An introduction to their probation period and what will be expected of them

YOUR BUSINESS

While it's important to give your new employee information that will help them to get off to a good start with you and help them see what your business is all about, you don't want to give them all the detail at once, and have them glaze over and lose interest. Stick to the key facts, the interesting stats, and focus on your customers: who they are, how great they are, and why it's so important that the whole team does their bit to look after them.

YOUR BUDDY SYSTEM

If you have a number of team members, it is always a good idea to appoint a buddy for the new employee at their orientation: someone who will guide them through their first few weeks and months, who will support them, act as a sounding board, and challenge them, as the need arises. This person will also introduce their new buddy to the Rules of the Game, explaining why you have them, how they work, and why they are important. The buddy system is key to embedding your new employee into your culture, applying, as it does, subtle and friendly peer pressure to behave in a certain way.

THEIR PROBATION PERIOD

In keeping with everything else about your business, your probation system should be clear, straightforward and professional, with supporting documents that tell your new employee everything they need to know.

By the end of their orientation, your employee will:

- Know how long their probation period will last.
- Have a document to take away to refer to at home, to show the family, to get excited about. A professional, clear and well-written document with no jargon or techy-speak, that indicates the suggested time-frame in which each element of the training programme should be completed.
- Understand that some of their training will be carried out on the job, some away from the workplace, and that there will be milestone checks of their progress along the way.
- Know that they are being assessed for their ability to learn and pick up skills; their attitude to learning; their ability to build relationships – with other team members, with you, with their buddy; their demonstrated values.
- Be clear that on X date at Y time, they will receive a formal probationary review from you, with their buddy present, at which they will learn whether they have met the standards of both be-haviour and attitude expected of your team. It is a good idea to give them a copy of the review at this point so that they know what to expect.

- Have signed a form to say that they have fully understood what is expected of them during this period.

The idea of the orientation, and particularly the discussion of the probation period, is not to stress out your new employee, but rather to set the tone and set out the standards in such a way that they are inspired to hit the ground running, and be an asset to your team from the off.

YOUR PEOPLE DEVELOPMENT SYSTEM

If you are serious about developing a strong reputation as an employer, then a formal and comprehensive development system which covers both essential skills for your business and personal and behavioural skills specific to the individual, is a must. Too many small businesses, and undoubtedly a number of large ones, carry out their training in a haphazard and unplanned fashion; making the time and freeing up the budget, only when needs must.

> **If you want your business to continue to grow, systemise your business and develop your people.**

If you want your business to continue to grow, and to be consistently good for your customers, you have to do two things: systemise your operation and develop your people. There are no short cuts;

there is no way around it. You simply must invest in your team.

The good news is that you have already invested time in working out who your ideal employee is, and you've made sure that you hired that ideal employee, so now, when you invest in their development, you can be pretty confident that it will be a long-term investment. The savings you will make from not re-hiring and not re-training will far outweigh the cost of developing the right employees.

The development process is made up of three parts:

- Initial Training
- Ongoing/ role-specific training
- Behavioural training

Initial Training

An employee's initial training plan will guide them through all the basic areas of your business, those areas that you want your entire team to understand and operate at some level. You will have a good idea of how long this initial training period should take, including time for the employee to practise and become confident in each area. Ideally, you will give them a schedule which plots their initial training, and also develop a spreadsheet that keeps an ongoing track of progress and logs training completed for this employee and all team members.

In each area, your new team member will be taught the basic systems, broken down into manageable and logical mini-systems. Ideally, there will be a crib sheet for each of the mini-systems covering the must-do elements of the role and, most importantly, the standards and values you expect all team members to live up to when performing the role. At the end of each small chunk of training, the individual will be quizzed, to ensure that they have picked up the key points, and understand the role.

This type of training is often done using the ABC method of training which is carried out on the job or side by side. It consists of three elements:

- **Attention:** Grab the individual's attention by telling them something interesting about the role they are about to learn: a key fact, or funny anecdote.
- **Breakdown:** Break the process down into manageable stages and walk the trainee through all the steps which make up each stage. Provide them with a crib sheet that also breaks down the process for them and that they can review at home or as needed, until they are fully confident.
- **Check:** Check that they've learned the key elements by asking them a few testing questions. If they are unable to answer, go back to the breakdown section until they understand and are confident.

So, for example, you may want your new starter to learn order-taking, which might cover how to answer the phone, how to sell, how to sell up, how to prepare the order, calculating the price for the customer, etc.

Your training session might run something like this:

Attention: 'Hi John, this morning I'm going to teach you how to take a customer's order. When I first joined the business we were only taking about three orders a day, but now we are up to 10 on average, and with you on board I'm sure that figure will grow even more!'

Breakdown: 'OK, so the process for taking an order is broken down into seven different stages. Let's start with how we answer the phone, which sets the tone for the whole conversation with the customer. The very first thing we do is… '

Check: 'Well done, John, you seem to have picked that up really well. Before we set you loose on a few live customers, let's just check how much you've remembered. No looking at your crib sheet...'

While very basic, this method of training works in many situations, even when the task to be learned is complicated, and if done well it does not need to be repeated.

Of course not everything can be taught on the job, and there will be skills that you want your employee to learn that may require either online or more formal training. How to spot Moments of Truth, how to deal with challenging customers, how to prioritise, are all examples of training which may require role play and discussion, and are therefore more appropriate for a classroom-style setting or external training.

If you do not have time to develop your own courses, there are numerous companies online, that will be able to help you.

Ongoing/Role Specific Training

An employee's development should not end when they have completed their initial training, although that will always be the temptation. They are now fully functional after all, and money is tight...

Nooooooo!

The more you invest in your team, the more value you will get back, not only in terms of their performance, but also through their engagement with your customers and their loyalty to your business. It is a key element in the development of your high performing team and also your employer brand, and it should have formed part of the brand promise you made to your new employee when you hired them.

An ongoing training budget should be as essential for you as a marketing or operational budget, and should be the last thing that you cut, my reasoning being that if you look after your people well, they will look after your customers well and build relationships with them, which means that customers not only stay with you, but refer you to others, which means that you don't need to spend so much time looking for new customers, which means that you can make savings by cutting some of your marketing budget! Makes sense?

Now that we've established that you will have an ongoing training budget, the main aim will either be to address particular behaviours that are lacking, or which you want to develop, or to give certain individuals skills, for a particular reason or in a specialist area – maybe to keep professional training/skills up to date.

The behavioural aspects may have been picked up during the initial training period, or discussed at a performance review. You may have someone who struggles to be part of a team, or who is poor at written communication, or who is lacking in self-esteem. Helping them to improve in these areas will certainly help your business but, more importantly, it will also help them to grow and develop as a person.

The specific skills required may be as basic as Word or Excel, but they may be more specialised skills to assist you in key roles such as Marketing, Finance or Human Resources. These specialist areas do require greater commitment from you in terms of time and money for study, and external verification, but developing your in-house skills in these areas says a great deal about your commitment to your team's development, and will save you a small fortune in hiring in these specialists (even more reasons to have a training budget).

In terms of the team and more values-driven training, I would recommend NLP (Neuro Linguistic Programming). Forget the awful name, which puts so many people off, NLP has a great deal to offer a business such as yours which wants to have the best possible relationships within your team, and between the team and your customers.

Individuals and teams who go through this training learn about the limiting beliefs that are holding them back, how to motivate themselves and others, how to be positive every day, how to build rapport and maintain it through great communication and body language – all of which would add enormous value to your business on a day-to-day basis.

Do me a favour and look into it, at least; I've recommended a few excellent trainers that I've worked with in the resource section at the back of the book.

THE COST BENEFIT

Businesses big and small quibble about the cost of training, and the time involved to complete it. It is often the first budget to be cut, if a budget is even allocated in the first place. And yet the benefits of training, of having a consistent process for

> **The benefits of giving everyone in the team the skills and understanding they need to do their job well, speak for themselves.**

giving everyone in the team the skills and understanding they need to do their job well, speak for themselves.

- Everyone knows their job
- Saves time and money correcting silly mistakes
- Everyone does things in the same way consistently
- A well-trained team delivers both quality and speed
- You don't need to be there for the business to run smoothly
- Your team are fully engaged because they are being developed
- Individuals feel empowered and take responsibility for their own job
- Individuals grow as people as well as employees
- Customers receive a consistently excellent experience

- Your people stay with you because they feel valued; saves money in hiring
- You trust your team more
- You save money because you are efficient
- You make money because you have a high performing team

Grow your people, grow your business!

> **"Surround yourself with the best people you can find, delegate authority, and don't interfere."**
> RONALD REAGAN

PERFORMANCE MANAGEMENT

No matter how good the people you hire, they will need to know how they are doing at any given point and to be kept on track. To a certain extent they will get this from ongoing feedback as they work, but they will also benefit from a much broader view of their overall performance and their progress within your business. This will be achieved through a performance management system.

Performance management is one of the most essential key People systems for any business.

It ensures that everyone knows what is expected of them and how they are doing against those expectations. It also helps *you* to know how everyone is doing and where work is needed to keep everyone moving forward together.

With a robust and consistent performance management system there can be no passengers, simply because there is no hiding place for them. Bad eggs are sorted quickly, and those who want to develop and learn are continuously motivated to do so.

What is a Performance Management System?

If you have never come across a performance management system before, it is a cycle made up of three parts:

1. The Performance Development Plan – goal setting
2. The Personal Development Plan
3. The Performance Review

Every employee will be introduced to the cycle at their orientation, when they are taught about The Rules of the Game, the required behaviours and competencies, and the support they will be given through the Performance Development System we covered earlier.

The cycle begins immediately, with brand new employees set basic goals which must be delivered in advance of their first performance review, the Probationary Review. Following a successful probationary period, the employee will then agree their performance goals and their personal development plan and the cycle continues, with reviews acting as the check and balance on progress.

How it works

A commitment from you is how it starts: a commitment to making the system work, to being consistent with how reviews are carried out, when they are carried out, how they are rated.

You set a regular time each year when reviews are carried out, and you insist that they are not put off for any reason other than fire or flood.

You coach your managers in how to deliver a motivating performance review or, if you don't yet have any managers, you spend that time honing your own skills.

You don't cut corners.

You don't allow a few scribbles on a piece of A4 to be enough; you will have a formal document, and you'll use it.

You don't just have a chat with an employee you know well. If this stuff is important to you, make sure *everyone* in your team knows that it is.

Better not to have a performance management system at all than to have an inconsistent or ad hoc process. This thing needs to work effectively and be consistent – and that comes from you.

> We are all far more committed to our own ideas, and to those things we challenge ourselves to do, than we ever are to those things that are imposed upon us.

The Performance Development Plan

The performance development plan is a working document which records the SMART goals you have agreed with your employee. I'm sure that like me, you've been brought up with SMART goals and understand the structure well, but just to recap, SMART goals are:

- **Specific** – answering the questions Who, What, Where, When, How, and Why?
- **Measurable** – have a means of measuring the result
- **Achievable** – not beyond the reach of the individual, but stretching them to improve their skills
- **Relevant** – to the individual, in the context of other goals, to the business
- **Time-bound** – have a target time/deadline by which the goal should be completed

The best way to create goals for an individual is to do it with them; getting them to come up with challenging goals for themselves with your guidance. We are all far more committed to our own ideas, and to those things we challenge ourselves to do, than we ever are to those things that are imposed upon us. The name of the game is to create a clear set of goals that you both believe are achievable with effort. Clarity is key; don't ever assume any knowledge in goal-setting.

Ultimately, the achievement of goals is down to the individual; they are responsible. *Your* responsibility is to commit to supporting them, to monitor their progress and to celebrate their little wins along the way.

One danger of basing your performance management system solely around the completion of SMART goals is that people focus too much on the What of achieving their goal, and forget about the How.

Doing the thing that needs to be done is not usually the hard part, it is *how* you do the thing that shows your qualities and skills.

I can bake a cake and I can paint a picture, but I can't bake a cake to the same standard as Delia Smith and I can't paint as well as Picasso. Also, in baking my cake I beat the bottom out of my bowl; in painting my picture I get paint all over the table and the floor. That should never be good enough.

I have worked with employees who have walked all over their team-mates, ignoring their requests for help and support, just to make sure that they achieve their goals; and others who have ignored their day-to-day priorities and work load, working on their goals at the expense of everything else. The How really is just as important as the What.

The performance management system focuses on developing the person as well as the employee and should therefore always be linked strongly to a set of expected behaviours and, of course, your Rules of the Game, so that nobody is in doubt that simply ticking the goal-completed box is not enough in your business.

Your expectations and measures of success will be made clear to your employees from the outset, and reiterated at each performance review. Ask your employee to play them back to you to ensure that they have a good understanding of both the quantitative (what, how many, how much, by when) and the qualitative (behaviours, standards, involving others, while still doing a good job) measures.

Ongoing Feedback

A performance management system does not remove the need for ongoing feedback. On the contrary, it makes it even more important and ensures that there are no surprises when it comes to performance reviews.

Clear and direct feedback which is both straight-talking and professional will always reap the greatest rewards. And don't be afraid to give it, even if it doesn't come naturally, or if your team member is sensitive. Everybody needs to learn.

If you've read *The One Minute Manager* by Ken Blanchard you will understand the power of investing just one minute to praise a team member for something you have seen them do well, or to reprimand them for doing something incorrectly and coach them to improve their performance. Both of which leave the employee feeling good about themselves and produce more valuable results. As Blanchard says, 'The best minute I spend is the one I invest in people.'

Be consistent with both your praise and criticism and you will reap the rewards for your business.

Building in the Customer's View

In a customer-focused business, building the customer's feedback into your performance management system is a great way to show your employees how important the customer's view is to you. On the basis of you get what you focus on, this is pretty much a no-brainer for strengthening your customer culture.

The customer's view also adds weight to the opinions that you have expressed in the review, and if you are able to include personal customer feedback about the individual being reviewed, it is immensely powerful in driving future performance. For those who need it, it also provides you with a great reason for collecting customer feedback in the first place.

The Personal Development Plan (PDP)

Your employee's personal development plan records those behaviours and/or skills that are not job specific, which are more personal to them, that you both agree they need to work on.

Initially the plan may include things like time management (because they are often late for work, or do not complete tasks on time) or assertiveness (because they don't speak up for themselves enough), or building relationships (because they are struggling with both team mates and customers).

Later in their development they may need help in report-writing, presentation skills or basic accounting skills, all of which broaden their capabilities and are of great benefit both to them personally and to your business.

The PDP is all about the needs that you have observed as their manager, discussed with them at their performance review, and it will cover the following:

- What area is to be improved or developed?
- What is the objective?
- What will be done to address this area (a course, a project, practical side-by-side training)?

- How will the outcome be measured?
- By when?

The Performance Review

We have already talked about the importance of committing to a set time-frame for formal and informal Performance Reviews. Obviously, how you decide to work the system is down to you, but I would recommend a formal Annual Performance Review supported by a formal six-monthly review and two informal, quarterly How's it going? chats.

If this sounds excessive, look at it this way: what in your business is more important and has a greater influence on the experience of your customers than your team? This investment is enormously valuable, not only for your customer experience and employer brand, but also for your bottom line. I encourage you not to underestimate its value.

> **What in your business is more important and has a greater influence on the experience of your customers than your team?**

Formal Reviews

For the annual and six-monthly review you will need the following formal documents:

- The Performance Review itself
- Guidelines for the competencies/qualities that you expect your employees to demonstrate, with examples of good and bad
- A rating system – for example 'excellent' through to 'needs improvement', with examples of what each looks like
- A Performance Development Plan, on which will be written the agreed SMART goals for the coming year
- A Personal Development Plan on which the employee will write the agreed steps that need to be taken to improve certain skills, or aspects of their behaviour

See the 'Need More Help?' section for more information about where to find these documents.

The time set aside for your team member's performance review should be sacrosanct for both you and them and, while it is important to have a rough time in mind for how long it will take, there should be no limits. This is an important investment of time, and it is vital that the individual has your undivided attention for as long as it takes to work through their performance issues and help them to see a way forward.

The best reviews are always those where the individual leaves the room feeling motivated to improve and develop their performance. Even when they have had a tough year, a good balance of what they need to build on and what they need to change, from you, can leave them feeling challenged but uplifted, and that should always be your aim. I have sat in on way too many reviews where the entire focus of the reviewer has been on the negative, and watched the employee visibly shrink under the onslaught. I have also experienced reviews where performance issues have been gilded over, and only the positives discussed. Neither extreme is of any value to the employee or the business.

Informal Reviews

Informal Reviews, or How's it going? chats, as they are often known, are not essential, but they are a great way of keeping an individual's performance moving in the right direction. Six months can be an awful long time to leave someone without a sit-down, one-to-one catch up, and an awful lot can happen in the intervening period.

Investing an hour or two with each team member in the quarters between the formal reviews will show them how important you feel they are to the business and how much you care about them as an individual. It will also give them the opportunity to raise concerns that they have, which you may not have picked up on, and perhaps give them a boost right when they need it.

Ultimately, every business is a people business, so why wouldn't you invest in your most important assets?

No consequences

One thing I have learned about performance management systems is that they have to matter. They have to mean something both to the organisation and to the individual, or they are worthless, a paperwork exercise that neither manages nor improves performance. Too many organisations boast proudly of having a performance management system because they have the paperwork that says that they do, but they cannot show any improvement in performance resulting from their system as it is not linked to anything good or bad for the employee. Put simply, there are no consequences.

In my corporate life, I worked for an organisation where there were consequences, good and bad relating to how you performed. Both manager and employee took the performance review seriously: they prepared for it every quarter, monitored progress regularly, were concerned enough about the outcome to get a little nervous before their review meeting even when they knew they had done well. There were consequences, and it mattered.

When I moved into the public sector things were different. Yes, there was a performance management system, yes paperwork was completed, signed off, filed, but there were no consequences. Do a good job, do a bad job, cruise along doing the bare minimum, it made no difference at all. There were no consequences, and the impact on both good and not so good employees was to take the edge off their performance.

If you're a lazy person and you realise that you can get away with being lazy, that while you may well have a few stern words said to you about you not pulling your weight, you will not lose your job and it won't even negatively affect your pay, guess what? You will carry on being lazy.

If you're a diligent, hard-working person and you see others getting away with shoddy work or laziness, doing less than you but being paid the same, you may not stoop to being less hard-working, but it will almost certainly affect your morale and your motivation. You will either lose your edge, become accepting of the situation or quit. And if enough good people quit because their good performance is not recognised, you could end up with an organisation full of lazy or demotivated employees. An overstatement? Perhaps. But is it worth taking the risk?

Your performance management system needs consequences. They don't have to be extreme, either positively or negatively, but they do need to be taken seriously and drive and reward both improved and outstanding performance.

Dealing with bad eggs

Even with the best hiring system in the world, the most effective performance development and management systems, and the most caring of teams and employers, bad eggs slip through. It's just a fact of life.

Your performance management system will highlight those who are under-performing and form the due diligence necessary to ensure that

A good performance management system will be key to the culture of continuous improvement within your business.

you do not end up with a tribunal on your hands when you decide to let them go. If this ever happens, I would recommend that you speak to a Human Resources professional before taking any action.

A good performance management system will be key to the culture of continuous improvement within your business. Your people will know from day one that they are expected to develop and improve themselves and to look for ways to improve the business, and that you and your team do not carry passengers. Their buddy will explain this to them at their orientation; their team mates will confirm this through stories of 'how it works around here'; and you will reiterate what is expected of them at their probationary review. It is a wonderfully virtuous cycle that has tremendous financial benefits.

> "Develop your people. Focus on their strengths. Then make high demands based on a person's strengths. Finally, periodically review their performance."
>
> PETER DRUCKER

RECOGNITION AND REWARD

So, here's a question for you: what do you focus on in your business, really?

What's your biggest priority?

What would your team say that it is?

Because that is what they will be focusing on, no question.

If you talk about being customer-focused, but only recognise those who save you money or waste it, then your team will know that your real focus is money.

If you tell your team that the customer is your number one priority and then openly slate a customer who gives you negative feedback, then they will know that your pride is more important to you than your customer's view.

If you talk about how important people development is to you, and then cancel training courses or performance reviews because money is tight or you are too busy, you are sending a very loud and clear message to your employees, who will lose trust in you and become demotivated.

No-one is fooled by those who talk the talk, but don't walk the walk.

Your recognition and reward system is another vital cog in developing your high performing team. Don't underestimate its importance.

The Recognition and Reward System

As you would expect, your more formal reward system will be most effective if it is linked to your people development and performance management systems, and to your business goals.

INDIVIDUAL REWARDS

On an individual basis, you may want to award a bonus to those who achieve the top rating for their performance reviews, or perhaps you will determine that annual pay rises will be linked to the rating individuals achieve at their reviews with top awards for those rated excellent or good, and no rise for those rated only satisfactory or needs improvement.

If you do not want to commit to financial rewards, there are a number of other ways to recognise both top performers and those making every effort to improve and develop their performance. Team Member of the Month, or Quarter, can be a very low cost alternative to promote team spirit and motivate individuals to raise their game. And how about flowers, chocolates, vouchers, tickets to a match or a concert – there's no end to what you can reward people with if you are prepared to get creative.

TEAM REWARDS

There are opposing schools of thought about the benefits of linking rewards to team competitions, pitting one team against another. As someone who has always played team sports I believe that healthy competition drives improved performance and, when the teams are made up of people from different areas of the business, it can be a great way to find out who the natural leaders are.

Team competitions encourage the strong to help the weak; with the added fun that comes with working as a close-knit team, they can create real momentum in your business. The competition itself does not need to be complicated or difficult to manage either. It can be as simple as the greatest number of positive customer comments for the individuals within each team, or the highest additional sales.

PUBLIC RECOGNITION

People like to be recognised publicly – let's be honest, we all do! And it's pretty easy to create the opportunities to congratulate and thank members of your team in front of their peers, in fact you probably have a few opportunities already.

It's great for the team if you have monthly communications meetings or quarterly business review meetings, and these are tailor-made for recognising the whole team, and any individuals you want to single out. Monthly or quarterly awards can be tagged onto the end of these meetings with little or no disruption to the business, and will be another good reason for all your team to make the effort not only to be there, but to listen to what is being said.

There is always something to celebrate, even during a tough year. There will have been a little win somewhere in your business that everyone in your team will want to know about, and it's important that they do, to avoid that downward spiral of despondency that can hit teams who are not doing well.

You see this all the time in sport: a team starts to lose a few games; it affects their psyche; they start to lose to teams they have previously beaten easily; their owner gets downbeat; their manager is downbeat... Pretty soon they believe that they will never win again. They only start to pick up when a new manager or a new owner comes in and shakes them out of this mindset.

Little wins are sometimes not that little. Celebrate them!

AN ANNUAL PARTY

You can have a lot of fun during business hours, and I hope that you do, but giving people the opportunity to let their hair down with their team, and with you, outside work, opens up a whole different level of camaraderie.

Holding an annual event with your team where they can dress up and boogie on down speaks volumes for your appreciation of what your team

> **Little wins are often not that little. Celebrate them!**

do for you and your business day in and day out. It is an investment of your time and money (and these things are never cheap) that will set you apart as an employer and show your team that you care about them as people, not just as employees. It's a great opportunity to have a bit of fun with your reward and recognition too.

Consistency

As with all of your systems, it's important that you are fully committed to a reward and recognition programme before you start one. Be sure that it is what you want to do, that your people and your business will benefit from it and that you will be able to keep it going once you start.

Build a robust system which covers all the bases in terms of your HR policies, making sure that anything that is linked to pay is properly set up with the involvement of the tax man, and be committed to the detail, particularly relating to timeframes and frequency. 'If you say you're going to do something, do it wholeheartedly', has always been my motto, and with rewards, that is essential.

Lack of consistency is often the downfall of good reward systems, and it is often a lack of consistency in how individuals within the team are rewarded that causes the problem. If you're going to give out awards, have consistent criteria for how they are won; make sure it's clear and simple and understood by everyone.

Don't fudge the system either, giving people who have never won 'a turn', or changing the system to make it fit. That said, it is very easy to put 'triers' off, if only those who are constantly top of the tree, are recognised. So don't forget to take time to recognise 'most improved', 'the best smile', 'best time-keeper' to keep everyone engaged and motivated.

From little acorns

Little things matter, a lot. Knowing your team, individually, is right up there with the most important. It scares me how many people don't know the names of everyone who works for them, and I'm not talking major multi-nationals here. Or worse, they can't be bothered to learn the pronunciation of somebody's name, so they don't just make it up, but give them a name like Bob, or Jane because it's easier for them to remember. Can you imagine how it makes an employee feel? It may even have happened to you, in which case you'll know all too well.

The best boss I ever worked with not only knew my name and how to pronounce it (you'd be amazed at how many variations people can come up with for the name Marianne), but also what family I had, what was important to me, what my dreams and ambitions were, what made me get out of bed to come into work. He invested the time to get to know me personally, and as a result, got the very best out of me.

Saying please and thank you may be second nature to you, but you need to make it second nature to everyone who works in your business, part of your internal and external customer culture. Thanking someone at the end of the day for the work they have put in for you sends them home knowing that you noticed what they did and appreciated their effort. It gives them another reason to want to come back in tomorrow.

Having a system for remembering birthdays and anniversaries, and then coming up with something personal to acknowledge the day – maybe letting the employee go early, or sending them flowers – will also cost you very little, and the payback will certainly be worth it in terms of increased loyalty and motivation. Don't make a rod for your own back with this one, though. Keep it simple, keep it personal and keep it consistent.

A great deal can be achieved by focusing on the simple and the personal rewards; throwing money at a reward system can sometimes have an adverse effect on motivation. I have seen family cultures destroyed by the expectation of financial payback simply for doing a good job, and petty jealousies create unhealthy competition and destroy what had always been a great team spirit. This is an extreme example, but it can happen.

Thoughtful, personal rewards will always mean more, even to those who really need the money and, like receiving a cheque instead of a Christmas present, the money is easily spent and quickly forgotten.

Keep it simple. Keep it manageable. Keep it consistent.

> "There are two things people want more than sex and money... recognition and praise."
>
> MARY KAY ASH

We said at the beginning of this section that your ability to control your costs around your People and your Operations will have real and significant impact on your business growth, profitability and cash flow. The best way to control these costs is by ensuring that you have simple and effective processes in place; processes that eliminate duplication and inefficiency, and engage your whole team in the delivery of a consistently excellent customer experience that is branded to you.

A high performing and productive team operating logical process and systems will not only deliver sustainable growth in your business, but will also give you more time, more control and more profit.

Take action now.

> "It is an immutable law in business that words are words, explanations are explanations, promises are promises but only performance is reality."
>
> HAROLD S GENEEN

5 KEY POINTS TO REMEMBER

1. A small change to an existing process can make a big difference.

2. Your first hiring question should be – do I need to hire at all?

3. The benefits of being a good employer show up on the bottom line and in the workplace.

4. If you want your business to grow, systemise your business and develop your people.

5. A good performance management system will be key to the culture of continuous improvement within your business.

If you do only one thing as a result of reading Part 3...
Carry out a 'brown paper exercise' with your team.

PART FOUR

Grow Your Business – Know Your Business

"There is no substitute for accurate knowledge. Know yourself, know your business, know your men."

LEE IACOCCA

KNOW YOUR OWN BUSINESS

Ask the owners of most small businesses if they know their numbers, and I guarantee that, to a man, or woman, they will say yes, because to most business owners the only numbers that matter are the top line or bottom line numbers: turnover, profit, cashflow and costs.

Ask them to dig a little deeper and they are all too often stumped.

- How many new customers have you taken on this year?
- How many customers have you lost?
- How many of each product or service are you selling?
- What is your ROI for each product?
- How many of your customers pay immediately/7-14 days/15-30 days/30+ days?

If we don't know the answers to questions like these, how can we know what is working and what isn't; what's making us money, and what is costing us more to get out there than is coming back; what our customers love and what they hate?

There is a well-known rule of business thumb – I like to call it the 'energy vs profit equation' – that says:

80% of your money comes from 20% of your business
15% comes from 40% of your business, and only
5% of your money comes from the remaining 40%

So, for example, if we know that an area of our business is expending 40% of our energy and delivering only 5% of our profit, but we are using it as a loss leader, or because we know that the product or service will start slow and grow, then all well and good. It is a strategic decision.

> **Understanding where you make your profit and where your energy needs to go to drive it, is crucial to your business growth.**

If, on the other hand, we have diversified because we think that's how to grow our business, and actually have no idea where each area of our business factors into the 'energy vs profit' equation, then we need to be taking a good hard look at those 80:15:5 ratios, to see if those products or services are worth the time and money we are investing in them.

Understanding this, knowing where you make your profit and where your energy needs to go to drive that profit, is crucial to your business growth.

Start with the Basics

Here's just a quick reminder of the basic financial documents that track the flow of money through a business.

The Balance Sheet lists your assets and liabilities, among other numbers, from the time you started your business, and gives you an overview of your financial strength and capabilities.

The P&L (Profit and Loss) Statement, lists your income (revenues or sales), minus your expenses, and shows you the profit or loss over a specific period of time.

The Cash Flow Statement helps you stay on top of how much money is coming and going through the business, and shows you why, even if your business seems profitable, you don't have much money in the bank.

Profit is a term that we all think we understand, but there are several terms which refer to the profitability which can sometimes cause confusion.

- *Gross Margin*, which can also be called gross profit, is the money you have left once you have subtracted the direct costs from the selling price of your product or service: your income minus your direct costs equals your gross margin. You want this figure to be good and healthy so that you have enough left over to pay your indirect costs or overheads (things like salaries, rent, marketing, telephone, and utilities) and still make money. Not having enough left over is a good indicator that your prices are too low.

- *Net income* or net profit is commonly known as 'the bottom line'. To get to this number you take away all your expenses, including tax, from your revenue. This money is what you will use to run your operation, so if it's negative your business isn't profitable and is running at a loss.

- *EBIT* (earnings before interest and taxes) is another way to report earnings for a business, but it can be deceptively optimistic due to the figures it *doesn't* take into account.

Creating your business dashboard

Once you have a good feel for your most critical numbers, and how to calculate them, you can then begin to work with them to understand the health of your business.

Creating a weekly dashboard that focuses on the key numbers for your business will help you to do this. It will also help you to monitor any potential problem areas and give you a basis for action.

It's likely to include some, if not all of the following:

Revenue: A comparison of your current numbers with similar periods in the past and, more importantly, with what you want them to be in the future: your progress towards a future target.

Net Profit: A view of how each area of the business is delivering profit – ideally with the 'energy vs profit equation' factored in.

Costs: A breakdown of your costs, particularly payroll costs and overheads, as a percentage of your sales will help you to spot trouble early, and deal with it. Any rise in these percentages should be investigated.

Cashflow: We always want to know that we have enough money coming in, to pay our bills, ideally with a bit of surplus for contingencies, and to have a good feel for money that we need to chase.

Total stock: If you keep an inventory in your business, it's something that you want to check on a weekly basis. Holding too much stock can be just as deadly for your business as holding too little.

Debt-to-Equity: As above, if your business has debt the figure belongs on your dashboard where you can keep an eye on it. At any given time you want to know your debt to equity ratio, and what you are comfortable with as a business.

Customer Experience: Knowing what has happened in our business from a customer's perspective is just as important as knowing the financial numbers. Have we taken on any new customers this week? How did they find us? Were they referred? Have we lost any, and if so, why? What social media comments have we received, good and bad? Any complaints?

You know what's most important to you and your business. Having this key information summarised on a one-page dashboard that is easy to review and becomes part of your weekly routine, will ensure that you know, and therefore grow, your business.

"When you control the ball, you control the score."
PELÉ

THE BUSINESS IMPROVEMENT PROCESS

For the long-term, to ensure that your business remains truly customer-focused and continues to deliver growth and profitability, you need something a little more robust and detailed.

In many ways, the business improvement process is your most important system, and is worthy of a book on its own. For now, though, let's just concentrate on the two basic requirements and how they can be set up for maximum business impact.

Business Process Review

To ensure that every process and system is working effectively, you will carry out a Business Process Review (BPR) once a year. While your business is still relatively small you may be able to do this twice a year, taking a day out of your schedule to check that your processes and systems are still lean and logical, that you are not duplicating effort, that they are operating efficiently. You will also take this opportunity to check both the progress being made and the standards being achieved through each system.

Examples of the sort of checks you would build into your review:

Hiring system – how many people have you hired; did they receive an orientation; what date was their probationary review; did they pass or fail?

People Development – has all initial training been carried out for each employee; are they up to date with their ongoing training; do they have an up to date Personal Development Plan?

Customer Experience – how many customers do you have; how many new customers have you attracted; how many referrals; have you lost any customers; what customer feedback have you received; any employees regularly receiving feedback, either positive or negative?

Performance Management – has every employee received an annual review; have they also had a formal six-monthly; how were they rated; have they made progress; are there any employees struggling or on monthly reviews as a result of poor performance?

Reward and Recognition – has your reward system been followed consistently; monthly awards given out; any special awards; annual awards given out; any one-off bonuses?

Financial Controls – how have sales fluctuated over the past twelve months; how well has each product sold; have you had any late-paying customers; how has cash flow fluctuated over the course of the 12 months; and profit?

Of course, for this review to be possible, you're going to have to keep good records throughout the year, something that should be built into your streamlined IT systems.

Your BPR day will provide you with a fount of information about what is working and what is not, and give you a fantastic helicopter view of your whole business.

Once you have all of the data together it will need to be analysed to determine why some areas of the business are working better than others; the root cause of any problems; and the low-hanging fruit that can be tackled immediately. You may decide that you want help with this, either internal or external, to ensure that the analysis is thorough and the output structured in such a way that it can easily be fed into your plans for the business.

PLAN 2 GROW

As your business grows, your planning process becomes increasingly important, and potentially more time-consuming, so it is vital that you allocate time for it in your calendar to ensure that it gets done.

You may want to involve key team members, and perhaps even a few of your customers and suppliers, to ensure that you have the broadest scope of views, opinions and ideas.

Ultimately, you are looking for ideas to take the business forward so, as a minimum, you will be brainstorming the following key areas:

PRODUCTS
- Are our products still the right products for our customers?
- Are our services still relevant to/required by our customers?
- How could they be improved/updated?
- How is our product superior to our competitors'/how could we make it so?
- What new products or services could we offer?

PROMOTION
- How do we communicate with our customers?
- How do we currently promote our products?
- How do we assess that these marketing tools are working effectively?

- How should we be promoting our products going forward?
- How can we improve communication with our customers?

PRICE

- What does it cost the customer to do business with us (in addition to the product price)?
- How can we reduce that cost?
- What value could we add for the customer?
- What special offers could we put in place?
- Should we make changes to our payment terms?
- Are our prices realistic in today's economic climate?
- Should we be raising the price for any of our products or services?

PEOPLE

- Armed with the output from your BPR...
- What areas of our people development and performance management need to be improved?
- What skills do the team lack?
- Who are the talented people that we need to focus on and fast-track?
- Who, if anyone, do we need to remove?

PLACE

- Where are we selling our product or service?
- Are we where our customers need us to be?

- Where is the best place to showcase our products and services for our customers?
- How can we improve this?

CUSTOMER EXPERIENCE

- Are we easy to do business with?
- Do our customers receive consistently quick, friendly and accurate service?
- What are our hot spots and danger zones? Can we eliminate them?
- How many customers have we attracted this year?
- How many through referrals?
- How can we increase this number?
- How many customers have we lost? Why? What can we do to get them back/prevent the same thing happening again?

Your brainstorm should be free-flowing and unrestricted, no idea is a bad idea on a planning day, and even the craziest of suggestions may have an element that is worthy of further discussion. This is your opportunity to think big and get creative. You're looking longer term here, ideally three years down the road, so stretch yourself and your team with thoughts of what could be.

By the end of your planning day you will have, at the very least, definite ideas to investigate further and an action plan of what needs to be done by when. If you are involving other people in your planning, which is recommended, you should also have a further date in your diary not more than two weeks down the line in order to maintain momentum. You can even call it Momentum Day!

3-1-Q PLANNING

At this next meeting, armed with your research, your financials, and a strong cup of coffee, you and the team will plot out the next three years, starting with the end in mind: determining your priorities for the business; calculating any investment that needs to be made in equipment or resources; thinking about what changes will need to be made to process and procedures, and how you will communicate and teach them to your people.

> A 3-1-Q planning process is a great way to keep momentum in your business.

Your focus initially will be on the long game, but over the course of the day you will focus in on what will be achieved in the coming year, the next six months and, finally, the next quarter. Everything should be documented, and a gannt chart (or largescale yearly planner) detailing work, projects to be delivered and milestones along the way should be posted where you and the rest of the team can see it.

A 3-1-Q planning process is a great way to keep momentum in your business and ensure that it is kept on track in terms of your customer experience.

You have the long-term 3-year view (and of course you can look further ahead if you feel it necessary or appropriate) that gives your team a vision for the future, for themselves as well as the business. The one-year view that tells them what the immediate priorities are, and what they will be delivering over the course of the year; and the short term stuff you've got to get going on now, with short term objectives and the opportunity for quick wins and the achievement of milestones.

Once a quarter the team who put the plan together will meet for a Momentum Day to assess progress and drive each other on.

Involving a specialist

If you are unsure where to start in setting up your business systems and your improvement process, it may be a good idea to bring in a specialist mentor who can support you with the detail and act as your Jiminy Cricket (or conscience) to ensure that dates don't slip.

The objective eye of someone who is not a stake-holder in your business will help you to see past the wallpaper of 'that's the way we do things around here' and help you to sharpen up your systems and processes. As you grow they will be useful in checking your progress and, as I mentioned earlier, helping you to analyse the data gathered during your systems audit day.

Involving the team

You'll have heard the old saying, 'None of us is as good as all of us'. The most successful teams are those in which every member has a part to play that contributes to the whole. How many times have you seen a team with less skilful players beating a team full of skilled superstars? They win because they *are* a team: they're all involved; they're all clued up on strategy and tactics; they all know their job; and they are all engaged and have bought into the ethos, values and spirit of their team.

> **The most successful teams are those in which every member has a part to play that contributes to the whole.**

Bringing together and drawing on the different skills, strengths, experience and ideas of your hand-picked team, your suppliers and your customers *will* enrich your business planning, and make your business more successful. The additional benefit is that your team will be more motivated and committed to plans that they have helped to shape.

Your people development system will ensure that everyone experiences each other's role, creating greater understanding of and empathy with one another, and also ensuring that no-one can pull the wool over anyone else's eyes! This in turn has the potential to create a bit of peer pressure if milestones are not being delivered by one individual or in one area of your business.

Delivering on plans that they've helped to create should be fun for your team. And it's your customers who will reap the benefit of better products, better services, more value for money, and enjoyable relationships with you and your highly motivated team.

SETTING THE STANDARDS

As you build or develop the systems I've outlined, you have a great opportunity to review the standards and the targets you have set your team, as your new systems will allow you to ask for more and achieve more.

SMART stretch goals will challenge and inspire your team, and engage them in the business. And, providing you have given them enough of the right resources – people, equipment, time – they will deliver for you.

A key element of any system is the measure of its success. As you design each system, decide what you are going to measure, what you are going to report on and how often (making it part of your business improvement process). You should have no reports just for their own sake: colourful pie charts and graphs can look impressive, but we are all about action here. If your report is not actionable, it is not necessary.

> **If your report is not actionable, it is not necessary.**

Celebrate the quick wins; celebrate the achievement of milestones; enjoy them, but don't allow your team to lose sight of the bigger goal.

Communicating the Plan

Regardless of how many of your team you can involve in developing the plan for your business, it is crucial that you communicate the plan to the whole team. Bringing everyone together once a year to talk to them about the wins and learns of the past year, and the plans for the coming year, will help to set the business up for success. You don't have to follow the John Lewis Partnership model of calling all your people Partners in your business, but you do have to make them all feel like they have a stake in the success of the business, and the best way to do this is through open and honest communication.

Regular quarterly or monthly communications meetings give you the opportunity to keep everyone engaged. Through updates and progress reports that are both visual and clear, in formats that everyone can understand and engage with, you will keep the whole team moving forward together and in the right direction.

By spelling out what needs to be achieved by when, you make everyone's life easier: they know where they stand, what has to be done by when, and they can just get on with it in the knowledge that they will be well rewarded for their efforts and achievements. Job satisfaction off the scale.

The business improvement process is a cycle, as long as you keep pedalling, it will keep your business moving forward.

As business owners we often rely too heavily on our accountants when it comes to tracking our numbers. And while a strong relationship with a good accountant is essential, we can't afford to forget that the buck stops with us when it comes to the financial health of our company.

The business improvement process is a cycle; as long as you keep pedalling, it will keep your business moving forward and growing in the right direction.

5 KEY POINTS TO REMEMBER

1. Knowing your numbers beyond turnover, profit and cashflow is crucial to your business growth.

2. As your business grows, your planning process becomes increasingly important.

3. A 3-1-Q planning process is a great way to keep momentum in your business.

4. Keep your team involved, keep them engaged and give them the systems that they need to help you deliver on your plans.

5. The buck stops with you when it comes to the financial health of your business.

> **"Without continual growth and progress, such words as improvement, achievement, and success have no meaning."**
>
> **BENJAMIN FRANKLIN**

If you do only one thing as a result of reading Part 4... Create a one page dashboard of the key numbers you need to be looking at on a weekly/monthly basis.

PART FIVE

Grow Your Business – It Ends With You

"Before you are a leader, success is all about growing yourself. When you become a leader, success is all about growing others."

JACK WELCH

YOU ARE THE LEADER: UNDERSTAND YOUR INFLUENCE

You will almost certainly have heard of the expression, 'The shadow of the leader', but have you ever considered the size of your own? How big the shadow is that you cast over your business. What qualities you bring, what things you do, how you do them, what your personal impact is.

Your authenticity is crucial to your success.

In your business your personal impact is huge, and that makes it a huge responsibility because there's another expression – 'A fish rots from the head'.

Your people watch you, they listen to you and they copy you. Your authenticity is crucial to your success.

What are you doing that others will see and interpret? What meaning could be attributed to your actions beyond the actions themselves? What could you do differently to signal new priorities or to better demonstrate your values?

Questions, questions, questions, and *sometimes* you are too close to see the answer, so don't be too proud to ask for help from an objective and unattached source to be sure that your shadow is a positive and not a negative source of power for your business.

YOUR BUSINESS CULTURE

The *Oxford Dictionary* defines culture as:

> *'the attitudes and behaviour characteristic of a particular social group'*

In the business world, it is best described as an intricate web of behaviours, attitudes and beliefs that exist within an organisation. The culture web below, devised by Gerry Johnson back in 1988, best illustrates for me what culture is all about.

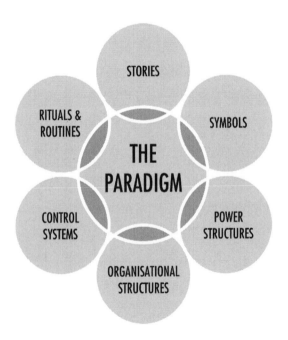

Johnson identified a number of elements that both describe and influence organisational culture:

- **The Paradigm:** what the organisation is about, what it does, its mission, its values.
- **Control Systems:** the processes in place to monitor what is going on.
- **Organisational Structures:** reporting lines, hierarchies, and the way that work flows through the business.
- **Power Structures:** who makes the decisions, how widely spread is power, and on what is power based?
- **Symbols:** these include organisational logos and designs, but also extend to symbols of power such as company cars.
- **Rituals and Routines:** meetings, reports and so on that may become more of a habit than a need
- **Stories and Myths:** build up about people and events, and convey a message about what is valued within the organisation (which may be very different to the one spoken about in mission and values).

Source: Gerry Johnson, original publication *Strategic Change and the Management Process*, Blackwell, 1987.

It's intricate and it's powerful and, in your business, you are its leader – what a responsibility!

> "Culture is a little like dropping an AlkaSeltzer into a glass – you don't see it, but somehow it does something."

HANS MAGNUS ENZENSBERGER

THE CULTURE BUILDING PROCESS

So where do you start? By looking at your culture as it exists now, and don't think your business is too small to have one.

Take a look at each of the elements of the culture web and, with notebook in hand, consider your business in relation to each. What does it tell you about the way your business culture is developing? Are you happy with the direction it's taking, or do you feel you need to make changes now, before it becomes entrenched? Do you see how much you personally have influenced the way your culture is growing?

To date, your culture has been evolving as a result of your day-to-day behaviours, words and actions. That's great news if you've been focusing on customer first, people development, reward and recognition, but even if you haven't there is still good news, because now that you are armed with this knowledge, you can set about designing the culture you want for your business.

Taking your lead

Culture evolves from consistent behaviours over time. Ask big companies who have tried to change their culture overnight whether a 'big bang' approach works, and they will tell you that it doesn't. Your culture will be built around your actions, your team's reactions and the truth about your business on a daily basis.

> Your culture will be built around your actions, your team's reactions and the truth about your business on a daily basis.

If you want a truly customer-centric business, ask yourself:

- How do I demonstrate that the customer comes first?
- Is it blindingly obvious that I love and respect my customers?
- Am I consistent?
- Would everyone who knows me say that I am?
- Would my customers?
- Are customers at the heart of every decision?
- How are decisions made?
- Who's involved?
- What questions are asked?
- Do I put myself in the customer's shoes?
- Do I think about the financial practicalities while remembering that 'good for the customer' should equal 'good for the business'?

If you are truly committed to your people's growth and development ask yourself:

- How do I show that I am?
- Do I invest consistently?
- Do I have a plan and a system in place?
- Would all my people past and present say that I care about them and their development?
- Am I paying lip service to my commitments, or am I 'walking the talk'?
- Do I do what I ask others to do?
- Do I talk to my customers?
- Do I always find win-win?
- Do I give immediate and constructive feedback?
- What are the Rules of the Game, and is everyone aware of them?

A business with a customer-centric culture will always have great feedback systems:

- What's my attitude to feedback?
- Do I listen?
- Do I *really* listen?
- Do I take time to read letters and e-mails from customers?
- Do I ask my team what they are hearing?
- Do I react one customer at a time, but watch for trends and the need to change a system?
- Would my team say that I welcome feedback and treat it as a gift?
- Would my customers?

- Do I use feedback as a stick to beat people with or as an opportunity to learn and do better next time?

The answers to these questions may shock you, or they may give you comfort; either way, the whole process of building a culture for your business will continue every day, whether you take control of it or not.

Engage your People

A strong business culture relies on the whole team buying into it. If you've taken your time in hiring the right people you will have no problem in engaging them in your vision and goals for the business, and in your culture. In fact, if you build a strong customer-centric culture, it will naturally spit out anyone who does not fit the mould: either they will leave of their own accord, or you will give them a gentle push, but they will go. I have witnessed this first hand in both the public and the private sector; culture is a powerful thing.

You have the right people, so involve them in finding solutions to problems, planning for the future, setting their own targets.

Immerse everyone in the culture from Day 1, building elements of the culture web into the orientation – the stories, the heroes, the rituals – showing through your actions what the culture is: arriving on time, everyone greeting the new starter warmly, choosing their buddy carefully to ensure that the shadow *they* cast is a positive one.

Explain the Rules of the Game to them, and demonstrate your personal values through everything you say and do.

Caring about the Individual

In the last couple of sections we've talked about hiring only those people who you are confident will love your customers, and then developing them so that they have the right skills and behaviours which engage them with you, your brand, and your customers.

One thing worth re-emphasising is just how much the success of all of this relies on you personally caring for each of your employees. Really, properly knowing who they are, what they want from their lives, why they are working with you, what they do outside work. Investing time in talking to your new employee about what they would be doing today if money was no object, finding out their dreams and then helping them to see how working with you could take them one step closer. Asking them what their hobbies are, what their sport is, who they support and then basing regular banter around it that shows that you have listened, will connect you to them on a very personal level.

No matter how big you get as a business, calling your people by their name (and with the right pronunciation) doesn't ever become less important. While you're still relatively small it's also a great idea to remember dates that are important too. Birthdays and anniversaries are the easiest, but also keep in mind the likes of Diwali, Chinese New Year and, of course, always look to celebrate the anniversary of your employee's start date with you.

While you can't always make decisions for the business based on individual needs, you can take into account your employees' needs before making decisions, and then communicate to the individuals about why, and how it might affect them. Even if something adversely affects one of your team, they will respect you if you have made the decision for the right reasons, for the majority and the continued success of the business, and will respect you for sharing your reasons with them personally.

Like everything else in your business, your employer brand starts and ends with you. You are the alpha and the omega, and all behaviours and actions that you witness in your business every day, can be traced back to something that you did or said, or didn't do or didn't say, that one of your team witnessed and remembered and believed it to be ok, and then either copied, or put their own slant on it. For good or bad, better or worse, that is the power and influence you have in your business.

"Earn your leadership every day."

MICHAEL JORDAN

Don't shirk the difficult stuff

Engaging with great people, be they customers or staff, is, or should be, easy. But, as we've already agreed, sometimes you have people who just don't fit your culture, your values or the ethos of your business and they have to go.

It's always good to give people a second chance, and I'm personally very big on forgiveness, but when a second chance has been had and wasted, don't delay in taking the appropriate action to remove the bad apple before it rots the rest of the barrel. The negative impact of someone who doesn't fit is simply too great and, in a growing business with a small team, you simply can't afford the consequences:

- For your customers, a poor experience.
- For your team, time wasted, frustration, the bad influence.
- For your business, potential lost customers and employees, ultimately lost revenue and profit.

And don't forget those bad customers too. You really don't have to hang on to customers who cause you stress, drain your team spirit, and/or don't pay their bills. Let them go and focus on those customers who are a good fit for your business values and your culture.

Say Goodbye Well

In the big scheme of culture and brand building, one element that is often forgotten by businesses big and small, but says a huge amount about them, is how they say goodbye to a customer or an employee.

Too often business owners take it personally when someone leaves them and get all bitter and twisted about it, when hopefully it's nothing to do with the owner at all, the individual has simply developed as far as they are able in the business and needs to move to better themselves. Whatever the reason, if someone leaves you congratulate them for their courage and ambition, give them a good reference and send them on their way with a farewell that they will always look back on with affection. Thank them for what they have done well for you and offer what support you can to help them to find a job that is perhaps more suited to them. Being kind and generous of spirit does not make you a mug.

The example you set in this regard will support the culture you are looking to develop, and help you to build an employer brand that people want to work for, and will speak well of when they no longer do. Money just can't buy that sort of reputation.

Communicate, communicate, communicate

Particularly while your business is still growing, you are your business, you are the leader, and people will want to contact you personally – both your customers and the individuals in your team.

> You are your business, you are the leader, and people will want to contact you personally.

How you handle this will say a great deal about you and your business culture.

Be open to contact: publish your telephone number on your website and literature; show up at networking events; spend time at the coalface working alongside your people. All these things will show that you care and give you access to priceless feedback.

But, be careful not to be too open! Remember that there are time vampires both outside and within your business who will suck you dry if you let them.

As in every other area of your business, build a system that controls the time you spend and gives you all of the advantages of regular and open communication while minimising the disadvantages. Consider the following as you look to build your system:

Telephone calls

- Hire someone to take your calls and schedule return calls into your diary as a block
- Set an end time for the call, communicate it (politely) and stick to it
- Make proactive calls to customers, scheduled into your diary, perhaps at the same time every week
- Once a month, schedule a time to take calls that your team would normally take
- Do a few callbacks to customers who have an issue

Face to Face

- Once a month/quarter, schedule a day where you visit customers
- Rotate who you visit and set yourself an objective for each visit
- Set a time in your diary every week as 'open door' time for your team

Sharing Information

- Share all but business-sensitive information with your team
- Hold communications meetings once a month to give and receive information
- Tell your team how business is progressing
- Let them know how they can help to make the business more successful
- Give them the information they need to do their job well
- Really listen to the feedback that your team give you, both verbally and non-verbally

Communication is vital in any relationship; just think how many marriages cite a breakdown in communication as a reason for divorce. Your business simply can't do without open and honest communication through channels that are clear and easy to use, so it's worth spending a bit of time with your team, and your customers, working out the best way to communicate with them.

> **"Communicate unto the other person that which you would want him to communicate unto you if your positions were reversed."**
>
> AARON GOLDMAN

LEADERSHIP PASSED ON

While you do not want to a team full of carbon copies of yourself, you do want people around you who naturally build strong relationships and who work hard to maintain them because they truly understand their importance and their benefit to the business.

Your people need to believe what you believe, to have the same values and standards, and to act as you would act when you are not around.

An argument rages about whether leaders are born or made.

Without doubt, I believe that some people are born leaders; they have a charisma and an energy about them that is not taught or learned. Some come from backgrounds where there were no positive role models and yet they still emerged to inspire and lead others.

Equally, though, I know that leadership behaviours can be learned. You can teach somebody to respect others, to be consistent, fair, direct and so on.

Indeed, charisma on its own, without the leadership behaviours to match it, can be a dangerous thing. Bill Clinton is a great example of a man with amazing charisma and energy, who was perhaps a little flawed when it came to being a leader. And there are many much worse examples.

Your culture is the soul of your business. Whether you want one or not, you have one.

Most good leaders I can think of have a strong sense of personal responsibility and accountability. It goes with the turf: you want to lead people, so you feel a responsibility to lead them in the right direction and do what is best for them. You become the least important part of the equation.

This is what I aim for with the people I mentor: to give them *all* the skills they need to be leaders. A team full of leaders is a powerful thing.

Your culture is the soul of your business. Whether you want one or not, you have one.

In a growing business, you are the heart and soul of your culture; you set the tone, you make the rules, you lead the way for your team to follow. As you grow, your team and your managers will build on the example you set, and your business culture will become a monument to the values and behaviours that you exhibit today – a powerful force in your business that will be difficult to change further down the line.

Day by day, action by action, you build your culture. Keep that in mind, and make it something you can be proud of.

5 KEY POINTS TO REMEMBER

1. Your authenticity is crucial to your success.

2. You can design the culture you want for your business.

3. Investing time with the individuals in your business will pay dividends.

4. Communicate, communicate, communicate.

5. You are the heart and soul of your business - you set the tone, you lead the way, day by day and action by action.

"A leader is best when people barely know he exists, when his work is done, his aim fulfilled, they will say: we did it ourselves."

LAO TZU

If you do only one thing as a result of reading Part 5... Be conscious of your behaviours today and lead 'on purpose'.

Conclusion

PASSION + PEOPLE + PROCESS = PROFIT

Throughout the pages of this book, I've asked you to assess what shape your business is in, your customer experience, your operational foundations, and your preparedness for growth.

I've asked you to step back and take a good, long, hard, objective look at your people, your systems and your process; to get into that helicopter with an imaginary customer alongside you and look down on their journey through your business, through their eyes.

I hope I've opened your eyes to the power of passion + people + process in the delivery of profit, and the necessity of all four coming together to make your business successful.

So where are you now?

At the beginning of the book I asked you to think about your top three problems in your business or life that you wanted to address. I also asked you to think about the things that were stopping you from getting to your ideal, whether real or imagined.

Take a look back at those now. Do you feel that you have the tools to solve your three problems?

Do those blocks still exist?

If you took the time to complete *The Business Review*, signposted in Part 1; if you completed it thoroughly, really thought about each area, searched for the information that you didn't have at your fingertips and took good notes, you will now have an excellent overview of where your business is currently, and where your areas of weakness lie. If you didn't complete the review, I strongly recommend that you do it now, while the rest of the information in this book is still fresh in your mind. Leave it, and we both know it won't ever get done.

What you do with the information from your review, coupled with what you have learned in the pages of this book, will determine the speed of growth for your business – perhaps whether you grow at all. It will also determine the sort of life you will have as a business owner.

You understand the foundations now, you have the knowledge and you're on the right track. But being on the right track is never enough; if you sit still you will soon get hit by a train. It is only movement and action that will build the life you want for yourself.

Act now. Take massive action. Take that first step towards the changes that will give you more time, more control and more profit. Start enjoying life, and your business adventure, again!

"The future depends on what you do today."

MAHATMA GHANDI

Thank You

Sincere thanks to you for buying this book – it would be of no relevance without you, and I hope it repays your investment in spades (not literally!)

Thanks to my publisher, Lucy at Rethink Press – persistent, patient and professional... everything you need to get a book to print. Thanks for (almost) removing my writing tic too... it's a better book because of you.

Huge thanks to KPI, particularly Daniel and Andrew Priestley, and Mindy Gibbins-Klein who inspired me to bring my dream of 'one day' writing a book to life. Thanks also to my KPI9 colleagues, and to the wider community of KPI who are a daily source of support and inspiration.

Thanks to McDonald's and all my friends there, past and present. Most of what I know about developing processes and leading high performing teams I learned in your company. Great brand. Great place to have grown up.

Thanks to Kim Rezk, whose enthusiasm, fun and friendship helped get Bright off the ground in the first place. You're one crazy, lovable lady!

Thanks to Liz Hopkin and Janette Eustace, associates and friends, who happily shared their knowledge and expertise, to help shape the content.

Thank you to my circle of friends and to my sisters – always there, always supportive.

Last, but not least, thanks to Sas for the love, loyalty, laughter and friendship that keeps me going, even on the less bright days.

About The Author

Marianne Page is Founder and Director of Bright, who specialise in liberating business owners by helping them to build a strong platform of logical, repeatable systems that give them more time, more control and more profit.

Marianne understands the powerful impact that simple and effective systems can have on a business, having had a successful and varied career with McDonald's for over twenty years, developing both process and people.

During this time, Marianne built systems which delivered both an outstanding customer experience and significant savings both corporately and for the many small business owners – the franchisees.

Having fine-tuned her skills in the challenging arena of the Health Service, Marianne set-up Bright, confident in the knowledge that her experience and expertise could help business owners to build on the model of Passion + People + Process = Profit, that has served her well, and seen McDonald's and other small businesses grow – often dramatically.

Now, with a team of specialist Associates to support her, Marianne is ready to liberate other like-minded business owners...one process at a time.

Marianne has spoken both in the UK and internationally on the power of process, particularly in relation to Customer Experience, and welcomes any opportunity to spread the message that Systems run the business; People run the systems.

Although based close to London, Marianne is proud of her roots in Consett, County Durham.

Resources

THE BRIGHT BUSINESS REVIEW

When you have good people and good systems, the systems run the business, and the people run the systems. This puts you in a strong position not only to grow, but should you wish to, to franchise your business. Good systems will transfer from unit to unit, town to town, country to country, and through a well thought-out performance management system, your people skills can also be transferred.

This review is designed to give you a high level snapshot of your business as it exists today. It follows the same path as the book, and asks you to examine:

- Your passion for, and role in your business
- Your customer experience and revenue generating systems
- Your operating and people systems
- Your knowledge of your business and financials
- Your culture and personal leadership

Set yourself aside a few hours, maybe a whole day, and go somewhere where you will not be disturbed to work through the questions and carry out the suggested actions. Take time to think about each area in turn; write down your thoughts and findings, perhaps using notes you have made as you've gone through the book.

The end game is to pull together a complete helicopter view of your four Ps (Passion, People, Process,

Profit) from which you can build a fifth, your Plan for business growth.

This Bright Business Review can also be found as a printable worksheet at www.bright7.co.uk/bonuses

WHERE ARE YOU NOW? IT STARTS WITH YOU...

What is your Passion Level?

- What do you value most?
- What kind of life do you want?
- Who do you want to be?
- What do you want to be said at your funeral?
- Are you doing what you love?

If you're not as passionate about the business as you used to be, what has to change to bring back the passion?

What's your Role?

Check out the roles below from Gerber's great book *The E Myth* and work out which role you are currently performing in your business and how it is affecting your passion, positively, or negatively.

THE TECHNICIAN

- Are you the Doer in your business?
- Are you the person who is very good at doing what your business does? (eg fix a plumbing system, mend a car, design a brochure, make a chair)

THE MANAGER

- Are you a pragmatist?
- Do you enjoy planning and organising?
- Are you predictable and systematic?
- Do you see problems?
- Do you bring order to the business?

THE ENTREPRENEUR

- Are you always looking for future opportunity?
- Are you always asking, what if…?
- Are you creative?
- Do you cause chaos in the business?

COMBINATIONS

- Are you the best combination – manager and entrepreneur?
- Or the worst – technician and entrepreneur?

Ask yourself what role you want to perform, and what has to change within your business for you to move into that role successfully.

How effective are your systems for revenue generation?

IS YOUR BUSINESS BUILT AROUND YOUR CUSTOMER AND AIMED AT SOLVING THEIR PROBLEMS?

- Do you have the right products?
- Are the product features still beneficial to the customer/up with the times?
- Do you have the right services?
- Is your service model up to date?
- Does each product or service still meet the customer's needs?
- How do you know? What is your proof?
    o What are your numbers…?
    o Referrals?
    o New customers?
    o Repeat customers?
    o Lost customers?

DO YOU FOCUS ON RELATIONSHIPS OR TRANSACTIONS?

- Do you build relationships?
    o How?
    o When?
    o What would your customer's view be?
- What is your view of your customers?
    o For life?
    o To pay this month's bills?

CUSTOMER EXPERIENCE

- Have you mapped your customer's journey?
- Do you know and manage your hot spots and Moments of Truth?
- Where are you leaving money on the table?

- Do your customers receive consistently good service?
- Are you easy to do business with?
- Do all of your people provide the same level of service?
- Are your systems built around the customer experience?
    o Review your customer feedback
    o Ask a cross-section of your customers for their view
    o Ask your team
    o Develop an action plan for improvement
- Do your systems cover every customer touchpoint?
    o From your initial message
    o To post-transaction feedback
    o Review your customer journey map
    o Develop an action plan for improvement

IS YOUR CUSTOMER EXPERIENCE PAINLESS?

- What do your customers tell you?
    o Directly?
        ▪ Through your feedback channels
        ▪ Socially
- By their actions?
    o How many have walked away?
    o How many have referred you?
- Is it painless in every area?
    o Observe
    o Look for patterns/trends
    o Measure improvements

- What are your hotspots?
    - Do you know?
    - How have they improved/ deteriorated?
    - Can they be eliminated?
    - Do you have an action plan?
- What is the team view?
    - Of their area?
    - Of the whole customer experience?

WHAT BLOCKS DO YOUR TEAM EXPERIENCE?
- How often do you ask them?
    - Do you have a system for their feedback?
    - Do you allow them to come to you?
    - Do you have a 'suggestion box'?
- Do you listen and monitor trends?
    - Is this a day to day activity for you/ for your manager(s)?
- Do you act on their suggestions?
    - And give them credit and thanks?
    - Reward them when it works?
    - Encourage more ideas?

HOW DO YOU COMMUNICATE WITH YOUR CUSTOMERS?
- Do you communicate with them the way they want you to?
- What marketing do you do?
- What other contact do you have with your existing customers?
- How do you communicate with them?
- How do your customers provide feedback to you?

- Do you ask for feedback proactively?
- What do you do with complaints?
- What do you do with praise?

WHAT FEEDBACK SYSTEMS DO YOU HAVE IN PLACE?
- Internal and External?
    - Employee opinion survey?
    - Customer complaints?
    - Mystery shopper/ caller?
    - Customer survey?
    - Performance reviews?
    - Face to face customer meetings?
- Consistently executed?
    - Planned into the business calendar annually?
    - Dates stuck to
- What do you do with the information?
    - Review your last twelve months (are you able to?)
    - What action have you taken after feedback?
    - What is your action plan for improvement?

HOW CUSTOMER-FOCUSED ARE YOUR PEOPLE?
- List all of your team
- Rate them for the following, from outstanding down to needs improvement
    - Customer relationships
    - Teamwork
    - Professionalism
    - Living your values

- o Desire for personal development
- o Risk taking
- o Work under pressure
- Review the ratings
- Are there any bad eggs? (more than two needs improvement scores)
- What is your action plan for dealing with those who need improvement?
- Do any of your team have skills that are under-utilised?
- Are any of your team great with customers until they are put under pressure?
- Are any of them 'on the right bus, but in the wrong seat'?
- What is your action plan for bringing the best out of these team members?
- Are your people following your lead?
- Do you demonstrate your customer focus every day?
- Is there anything that you have allowed to fall away in the past year?
- What is your action plan to get yourself back on course?
- What is the first step?
- What will you have achieved by the end of the week, the month?

Your business survives and thrives through your good relationships with your customers, your team and your suppliers.

How you live your values with all three and how you listen to and act on their feedback will determine the growth and success of your business

How efficient are your operational and people systems?

FORMULA ONE OR WACKY RACES?

From your helicopter viewpoint, answer the following:

- Is your operation well-drilled and smooth?
    - o   Systems control potential chaos
    - o   Nothing is left to chance
    - o   There is a process for every aspect of the operation
- Does everyone know their role?
    - o   Everyone in the team is working through your training programme
    - o   Everyone receives the same training
    - o   Everyone knows how the role they are performing fits into the overall system
- Is everyone working as a team?
    - o   Team members are trained to be able to cover every role in the business
    - o   Everybody knows how one role affects/supports another
    - o   The team have fun together
    - o   Everyone is professional in everything they do

OPERATIONAL

- Is your business 'set-up' to perform effectively?
  - Are your processes logical?
  - Is there any duplicated effort in your system?
  - Do your IT systems link together in support of your operation?
  - Do you find yourself double-entering information?
  - Do you do a travel path at the start of every day?
  - Do you set daily and weekly targets for your team?
- Do you have logical systems in other key areas of the business?
  - Marketing
  - Communication
  - Billing/Finance

PEOPLE

- Do your people systems add value?
  - Hiring
    - How many people have you hired this year?
    - What hiring system did you use?
    - Were you fully involved?
    - Did the new starter have an orientation?
    - Were they assigned a buddy?
    - Are they still with you?

- People Development
  - Is your training up to date and recorded?
  - Are your people developing as you would expect?
  - Are they engaged?
  - What is your action plan for your people development?
- Performance Management
  - Has every team member had at least one performance review in the past 12 months?
  - Were these reviews inspirational?
  - Do your reviews make employees feel valued?
  - Does every employee have a personal development plan?
- Reward and Recognition
  - How have you linked performance to reward?
  - Do you recognise good performance every day?
  - Have you set up awards to recognise performance on an ongoing basis?
  - Review what you have actually done over the last twelve months to reward your team.
  - Was it consistent and fair?
  - Was it well communicated?
  - Did you take every opportunity to catch your people doing the right things?
  - What is your plan for the next 12 months?

How well do you know your business?

SALES AND PROFITABILITY

- What was your turnover in the last 12 months?
- What was your profitability?
- What streams of income do you currently have?
- What proportion of profit does each contribute?
- What proportion of operating time does each consume?
- What proportion of the Marketing budget is assigned to each?

CUSTOMERS

- How many regular customers do you have?
- What services do these customers use?
- How many one-off customers have you had in the past 12 months?
- How many customers have you lost?
- How do you know?

FINANCE/ACCOUNTS

- What payment systems are in place for customers?
- What about suppliers?
- What issues do you have with cashflow?

MARKETING

- How do you market your business?
- What is your marketing budget?
- How do you determine what to market, and when?
- How much time do you/ your team spend annually on promoting the business?

TECHNOLOGY

- What software systems do you use to support your business?
- How does each system integrate/ communicate with the others?
- How many data sources do you have?
- Is your IT system still fit for purpose?

PRIORITIES

- What areas are you happiest with within your business?
- What keeps you awake at night?

What are your Goals?

Have you asked questions like those below to elicit top line SMART goals for your business?

PRODUCTS

- Are our products still the right products for our customers?
- Are our services still relevant to/required by our customers?
- How could they be improved/updated?
- How is our product superior to our competitor's/how could we make it so?
- What new products or services could we offer?

PROMOTION

- How do we communicate with our customers?
- How do we currently promote our products?

- How do we assess that these marketing tools are working effectively?
- How should we be promoting our products going forward?
- How can we improve communication with our customers?

PRICE

- What does it cost the customer to do business with us (in addition to the product price)?
- How can we reduce that cost?
- What value could we add for the customer?
- What special offers could we put in place?
- Should we make changes to our payment terms?
- Are our prices realistic in today's economic climate?
- Should we be raising the price for any of our products or services?

PEOPLE

- What areas of our people development and performance management need to be improved?
- What skills do the team lack?
- Who are the talented people that we need to focus on and fast-track?
- Who, if anyone, do we need to remove?
- How many people in your team? By when?
- How many fully trained? By when?

PLACE

- Where are we selling our product or service?
- Are we where our customers need us to be?
- Where is the best place to showcase our products and services for our customers?
- How can we improve this?

CUSTOMER EXPERIENCE

- Are we easy to do business with?
- Do our customers receive consistently quick, friendly and accurate service?
- What are our hot spots and danger zones? Can we eliminate them?
- How many customers have we attracted this year?
- How many through referrals?
- How can we increase this number?
- How many customers have we lost? Why? What can we do to get them back/prevent the same thing happening again?

FINANCIALS

- How much profit? By when?
- Business Growth – How much? By when?
- Sell business by…?

BUSINESS IMPROVEMENT

- Do you do a Business Process Review to keep your systems on track?
- Do you make time religiously for your annual planning cycle?

- Do you involve your team/a specialist?
- Do you communicate the plan to the whole team?

CULTURE AND LEADERSHIP...IT ENDS WITH YOU!

How involved are You?

- Do you show that you care about standards?
    - o Do you give immediate and constructive feedback?
    - o Do you never walk past a problem?
- Do you know how consistent your process is?
    - o What is the feedback from your team, from customers?
    - o What have you witnessed?
- How do you measure consistency?
    - o Customer satisfaction measures?
    - o Against improvement targets?
- Are you involved in process improvement?
    - o Is it part of your overall Business Improvement Process?
    - o Do you always make time?
- Do you listen to your team's views?
    - o As part of your review system?
    - o Through an employee survey?
    - o During the planning process?
- What is your customer's view?
    - o Review feedback
    - o Pick up the phone now and ask them
- Are your leaders effective, including you?

- o How did your leaders fare in the team review you did earlier?
- o What do you observe about them?
  - Customer interaction
  - Team respect
  - The same, day to day
- What input do they need?
- What is your action plan for improvement?

PLAN 2 GROW

Your business review will have given you a great deal of food for thought, and may well have thrown up more questions than answers.

Take the time now to review the major challenges you face, and to prioritise those areas needing most immediate attention/further investigation (red), those less urgent, but still in need of some action on your part (amber), and those that you are reasonably happy with, that only need to be monitored as part of your ongoing business improvement process (green).

Once you have done this, plan your action – what you will achieve, and by when. Plan what needs communicating to your team, and how you will involve them in making the necessary improvements. Then take that first step towards improving your operation. Do it now. Do not put it off until tomorrow.

Good luck!

RECOMMENDATIONS

NLP Trainers

TOBY AND KATE MCCARTNEY
http://www.tobyandkatemccartney.com

BEYOND NLP
http://www.beyondnlptraining.co.uk

STEVE AND DEB ADAMS
http://www.lifechangeconnection.com

Web design and Social Media Contacts

ASPURIAN
http://www.aspuriandigital.com

THE LOOP DIGITAL
http://www.the-loop.com

GREEN UMBRELLA
http://www.green-umbrella.biz

Further Reading

The Culture Web by Gerry Johnson, original publication Strategic Change and the Management Process, Blackwell, 1987

The E Myth Revisited by Michael E Gerber, Harper Business 1995

The Go-Giver by Bob Burg and John David Mann, Penguin Books 2007

Need More Help?

A BRIGHTER YOU

Bright was founded to help business owners just like you to step away from working in your business, and give you time to work on it. Marianne and her team of associates specialise in reviewing the way your business currently works, removing the inefficiencies and the bottlenecks in your process and systems, and delivering a programme of continuous improvement and a robust foundation on which to grow your business.

For more information about how Bright can help you to have more time, more control and more profit, book a free discovery session via

E-mail: info@bright7.co.uk
Tel: +44 (0)1234 881660
Web: www.bright7.co.uk

BONUS MATERIAL

Please make sure that you check out your five 'Process to Profit' bonuses and the training materials listed below. They're the best way I know to get you started. For instant access go to www.bright7.co.uk/bonuses

Bonus #1 Process to Profit Illustrated Book Summary

Download a full colour pdf illustrating the key messages in this book. Printable to A3 poster size – ideal for your office wall.

Bonus #2 Bright Business Review

Download the template to complete your Bright Business Review.

Bonus #3 The Rules of The Game

Download a full colour template of The Rules of the Game and adapt it to your business.

Bonus #4 The Brown Paper Exercise

Download full instructions for completing the Brown Paper Exercise in your business.

Bonus #5 Performance Management Templates

Download templates of the 3 key documents you will need for your performance management system.

BRIGHT IN A BOX – PROCESS BUILDER

'Bright in a Box' is a series of DIY toolkits aimed at introducing you to the benefits of simple, effective and logical process and systems within your business. Each box builds on the previous information to grow your knowledge, and provide you with the practical 'how to' of process building, including worksheets, templates and examples.

Developed by those who work practically with these tools every day, this Bright in a Box series is a must for anyone who wants to improve their operation, but does not want to call in specialist help.

For more information visit www.bright7.co.uk

Wishing you all the very best
for the growth of your business!